Negotiating partnerships

Increase profits and reduce risks

FINANCIAL TIMES

Prentice Hall

In an increasingly competitive world, it is quality
of thinking that gives an edge – an idea that opens new
doors, a technique that solves a problem, or an insight
that simply helps make sense of it all.
We work with leading authors in the fields of
management and finance to bring cutting-edge thinking
and best learning practice to a global market.
Under a range of leading imprints, including
Financial Times Prentice Hall, we create world-class
print publications and electronic products giving readers
knowledge and understanding which can then be
applied, whether studying or at work.
To find out more about our business and professional
products, you can visit us at www.business-minds.com
For other Pearson Education publications, visit
www.pearsoned-ema.com

Pearson Education

Negotiating partnerships

Increase profits and reduce risks

KELD JENSEN AND
IWAR UNT

FINANCIAL TIMES
Prentice Hall

An imprint of **Pearson Education**

London · New York · San Francisco · Toronto · Sydney
Tokyo · Singapore · Hong Kong · Cape Town · Madrid
Paris · Milan · Munich · Amsterdam

PEARSON EDUCATION LIMITED

Head Office:
Edinburgh Gate
Harlow CM20 2JE
Tel: +44 (0)1279 623 623
Fax: +44 (0)1279 431059

London Office:
128 Long Acre
London WC2E 9AN
Tel: +44 (0)20 7447 2000
Fax: +44 (0)20 7240 5771
Website: www.business-minds.com

A Division of Financial Times Professional Limited

First published in Great Britain in 2002

ISBN 0 273 65659 7

British Library Cataloguing in Publication Data
A CIP catalogue record for this book can be obtained from the British Library.

10 9 8 7 6 5 4 3 2 1

Typeset by Pantek Arts Ltd, Maidstone, Kent
Printed and bound in Great Britain by Biddles Ltd, *www.biddles.co.uk*

The Publishers' policy is to use paper manufactured from sustainable forests.

About the authors

Iwar Unt. When you talk about negotiations and training of negotiators, the name Iwar Unt always comes up. In Sweden he is called 'The father of the negotiation technique'. It was in the 1970s when he was working on some very important assignments for SAAB and Volvo that Iwar began looking at how these companies handled their purchase negotiations. Partnership negotiations were not practised at that time, neither within the car industry nor within any other sector. Iwar Unt began to question the procedure used, and he could quickly show that instead of fighting, the parties could create significant added values through openness, creative problem solving and dialogue. The partnership model has been developed over the years and incorporated as a fixed part of many companies. Many of the actors in today's business life do not accept other types of negotiation than the partnership model. They know their own value, expect to be treated with respect, met by openness and to get a share of the added values which they take part in creating.

Iwar Unt has been working within most sectors, and he has worked with all the parties around the negotiation table, from boards to the individual negotiator, buyer, seller and project manager. As negotiator and consultant he has solved many different negotiation problems with great success.

Iwar has written a number of books on partnership, negotiation technique and the creation of added value, and these books have been published on the Scandinavian markets, Great Britain, China and the United States.

Keld Jensen. Keld Jensen is a partner in and CEO of MarketWatch Management, an independent Scandinavian network organization. Through its strong base in the Nordic reference platform

MarketWatch works to motivate and develop companies' business growth across functions, sectors and professional and industrial bodies. The organization is exclusively focused on the core areas; the negotiation technique and related communication and consultancy within the same.

Keld Jensen has more than 13 years' management and negotiation experience. As idea generator and CEO of small organizations as well as listed companies, he has developed people, projects, products, participated in due diligence, company acquisitions and sale by means of which he has further developed his human resource ideas.

Through his work in MarketWatch Management, Keld Jensen has recently been co-author of the books *Negotiation Technique* and *The Negotiation Handbook*, and has offered professional advice and trained a wide range of leading international organizations, including ABB, Scandic Hotels, Ernst & Young, PricewaterhouseCoopers, Volvo, Rolls-Royce, Swedish Postal Service, BP Amoco, IKEA, SAAB, ERICSSON, Phillips, AstraZeneca and Mölnlycke.

"As I hurtled through space there was only one thought on my mind – That every part of the capsule was supplied by the lowest bidder"

John Glenn

Acknowledgements

I owe a debt of gratitude to my partner Mr. Iwar Unt for encouragement and insight into the negotiation of partnerships. Without his knowledge, experience and trust, I would never have found the 'new way'.

Our largest debt of gratitude must go to the thousands of people and clients worldwide that have participated in conducting our surveys and realising our theory into practice. As in real partnerships, without them, nothing could be done.

This and several other projects could only succeed with the support of my wife Liliana and my daughter Nadine. Without my home-based motivational team, I would probably have crashed on the way.

Keld Jensen

Contents

Introduction

Many people talk about partnership but are thinking predominantly about cost savings.

This book is based on experience gained through our meetings with more than 22,000 negotiators. During the 25 years in which we have been working as negotiation experts, our conviction that partnership is better than fighting has grown even stronger. Today many people speak of the win-win method but few master it fully. Our research shows that there are many fiascos that can trap us. Following the progress of business mergers all over the world will show that most of them fail. The human factor upsets the applecart. Many companies talk about partnership but only have a price reduction in mind.

This book addresses the hundreds of thousands of negotiators in business and administration who face different forms of negotiation daily. Today many are looking for a better alternative to the pure zero-sum game. It is our objective to disseminate knowledge that can be put into practice. 'Knowledge' used in the proper way, will mean that one party's advancement doesn't have to be at the expense of the other. Contemporary business practices can be humanist and meet demands for high ethics.

People who initiate a change in some form of activity are looking for long-term and stable relationships, relationships from which both parties benefit. In all cases, they hope that a partnership will provide them with better solutions than those currently available to them. They aim to reduce costs and risks, to improve earnings and to reap the benefit of each other's experience and contacts.

Go back a few years and look at what a typical company was doing in order to improve productivity or decrease costs. They were cutting overheads, reducing staff and management, redesigning processes, improving products and communications, and automating routine functions.

What did all these actions have in common? They were about *changes* within the company and its functions.

Very few organizations through their process of increasing competitiveness looked outside their borders. Many companies have come to realize that this is not enough. One survey pointed out that less than ten per cent of an average manufacturing company revenue is overhead.

In comparison, the average company pays more than 55 per cent of its revenue for goods and services. In other words, more than half of a company's revenue is spent on purchases outside the company!

Just help yourself

This might sound like a challenging invitation but the fact is that in many negotiations, there is a large and unexploited potential that may consist of:

- the traditional scope for negotiation defined as the difference between the highest price a buyer can pay and the lowest price a seller can come down to;

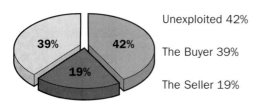

Unexploited 42%

The Buyer 39%

The Seller 19%

- the added value that the parties can achieve through negotiation by modifying the content and the structure of the agreement.

In many transactions, there is a great deal of unexploited potential. The negotiators who have learned how to identify these opportunities stand good chances of concluding better deals, and of doing so without making the other party feel like a loser.

When 2 + 2 = 7 and creates a partnership

In the jungle, the stronger presides over the weaker. The same can apply in the business world. But dictating terms and exploiting the weaknesses of the other party *ad absurdum* is not a very forward-looking solution. Not even to the party who reaps an immediate advantage from a display of strength.

The objective of partnership is to identify, develop and safeguard the added value realized — added value which means that the business can develop and grow, that there is a bigger cake to share. You have to test the limits and find the solutions in a businesslike manner and try to secure as much as possible for yourself. You should win the negotiation without leaving the other party feeling like a loser.

Co-operation and partnership do not presuppose sharing equally. It is your job as a negotiator to try to ensure that you can keep to yourself most of the added value created, but at the same time, you want the other party to be satisfied. In order for this to happen, the following criteria will have to be met.

- The other party must be able to manage and develop his business with the terms reached in the negotiation. He must continue to be a good and valuable partner.

- The result must offer him a better solution in relation to his other alternatives; a deal that he cannot afford to miss; a deal he would wish to uphold and protect.

- He must feel that it is a good deal and that he has performed well in the negotiation. He should feel that he has succeeded in his task.

A systematic search for the added value may yield new solutions which will more easily meet the needs of both parties. If they both have a bigger cake to share, it will be more likely that they will be able to find a division which is acceptable to both of them. A partnership with two satisfied parties may emerge, a partnership where neither of them needs to waive their demands to get a sound business deal through.

Partnership, or partnering as it is also known, is characterized by a constructive dialogue. The basis of co-operation is trust and openness. You should be generous to your partners and share any gains with them. If you keep too much to yourself, there is no incentive for innovation, creativity, burden sharing or wholehearted effort.

Some people do not accept the theory. They are convinced that fighting will provide them with the best chances. Sooner or later financial reality will force them to accept partnership as a basis for business. If not, their own bankruptcy will remove them from the market. This has even happened to communism — there is often a change of heart under the gallows.

A negotiation should be a constructive dialogue, a partnership in which the parties can benefit from each other's experience and resources to create added value between them. One party should not thrive at the expense of the other.

The terms, 'co-operation' and 'partnership' should not be seen as stylistic methods in which the purpose is to find solutions where both costs, responsibility, results and risks are equally shared.

This is not a theoretical book on mergers or strategic alliances' addressed only the chosen few. The book is about the human factor, what it is that leads so few to succeed and so many to fail in their attempts to establish a partnership.

Partnerships/partnering rewards those companies who can get beyond traditional ways of conducting business, and punishes companies who cannot get outside the traditional mindset.

Where are the opportunities, why is it that some succeed while so many fail? Read on and find inspiration.

We all want the best possible value for money. The buyer wants a Rolls-Royce for the same price as a Volkswagen. The seller delivers a Volvo but charges for a Mercedes. Life is one big bazaar where everything can be bought and sold, something which George Bernard Shaw tried to prove by negotiating with his dinner partner:

"Would you sleep with me if I gave you 100,000 pounds?"

"Why not? You are an attractive man."

"But I can only afford to pay 10 pounds."

"Rude! What do you take me for?"

"We have already established who you are, now we are negotiating about the price."

If you want to succeed better than Shaw, you will need common sense and tactics. The tactics which we present can also be used on other negotiation variables than price. The tactics which you can make use of or become subjected to vary whether you are seller or buyer.

To facilitate reading we shall use the pronoun 'he' in the rest of the text. Of course it signifies 'she' as well as 'he'.

Keld Jensen and Iwar Unt
Stockholm and Copenhagen

1
The gospel of partnership

Mergers

The winds of change are blowing all over the world. Everywhere the talk is of mergers, partnerships, and different types of co-operation in order to meet growing demands for profitability, efficiency, and competitiveness. Is partnership the golden solution, then? A study published by *The Economist* in January 1999 shows how difficult it is. Two out of three mergers failed in 1998. On paper and in the calculations on which co-operation is based, it is far too easy for managers to calculate their way to cost reductions and improved efficiency. In theory, it is easy to create added value. All you need is to mix the good old art of engineering with creative thinking, put all the pieces of the jigsaw puzzle on the table and take advantage of economies of scale. Some people would even take rational thinking so far that they leave it to the computer to calculate its way to the best conceivable solution. One added value after another appears on the screen. In real life, only very few people manage this feat: all too often the human factor contributes to the loss of most of the potential added value.

The number of mergers over recent years has increased by nearly 30 per cent, and the average value of each individual merger over the last five years has more than trebled to more than $100 million. And all the signs indicate a continuing trend.

The total value of international mergers and acquisitions reached $720 billion in 1999, according to the *World Investment Report* (2000) from the UN Conference on Trade and Development. Measured as a share of world GDP, cross-border mergers rose in value from 0.5 per cent in 1987 to over 2 per cent in 1999.

Riding the cost
Value of global mergers and acquisitions $trn

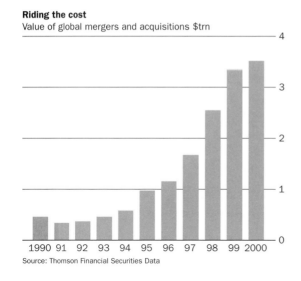

Source: Thomson Financial Securities Data

If you read the monthly merger and partnership reports in business magazines, the international list is as long as your arm, and each month values to the tune of billions are represented.

British companies are one of the biggest spenders. They spent some $254 billion on foreign mergers and acquisitions in the first half of 2000. This is more than double the amount of number two, France, which replaced the USA.

Strategic alliances, mergers, and partnership are keywords in the world of business today. Curt Nicolin, who was in charge of the merger between ASEA and Brown Bovery, makes a concerned statement in an interview with the leading Swedish newspaper *Svenska Dagbladet* on 17 November 1999; he sees the flood of mergers sweeping over the Western world as a fad rather than as an expression of economic reason. In order to improve their competitiveness, everybody is looking for new partners. Rumours in the spring of 1999 that Volvo was tarting itself up in an attempt to find a partner who would make a bid for the company made share prices go through the roof. This happened before anyone had had time to carry out any sort of financial analysis. Everybody simply assumed that huge profits were up for grabs.

Usually, the only winners are those off-loading because they get more money for their company than it is really worth. Robert Solov, Nobel Prize winner for economics for 1987, said to the *Svenska Dagbladet* on 25 August 1999: 'Only to a very limited extent do mergers contribute to improved productivity and profitability. Mergers mainly benefit the financial engineers who were behind them'.

So is partnership simply a sophisticated capitalist ploy to make the smart and strong even richer? Shouldn't a correctly designed partnership leave us with two winners?

The EU is in the process of negotiating the admission of new Member States. MD Foods crosses milky borders with Arla in Scandinavia, to become the largest in Europe. Halifax and Bank of Scotland have joined forces. There was a bid for the London Stock Exchange (LSE) from the OM Group, the Swedish company that owns the Stockholm exchange. GE tries to takeover Honeywell. Vodafone takes over German Mannesmann. The telecom corporations in Sweden and Norway Telia and Telenor negotiate with each other for a long time about joining forces before the whole thing comes a cropper on the finishing line. Volvo tries to take over Scania. Danisco merges with Cultor. SmithKline Beecham and Glaxo Welcome becomes GlaxoSmithkline PLC. Unibank merges with MeritaNordbanken, Hilton acquires Scandic Hotels and so on. We hear about one restructuring after another because companies want to become more competitive. Banks, vehicle manufacturers, airlines, insurance companies, pharmaceutical companies, and telecommunication operators; the list of industries in which companies are merging or initiating comprehensive co-operation is long. Economies of scale, conquest of market share, high development costs, co-ordination gains and increasingly difficult competition accelerate this development. More and more actors are spreading the gospel of partnership. Is this just another fad, or is it really a tidal wave carrying with it everything it meets on its way?

The problem isn't to carry out a theoretical calculation of costs saved and profits increased. The problem arises when reality has to be changed and gains realized. Experience shows that generally the human factor is insufficiently considered. In January 1999 *The Economist* wrote that the truly serious problems normally crop up in the 'soft' areas. Employees from companies with completely different corporate cultures suddenly have to work together. Strange people are entering their territory claiming parts of it or threatening to take over. The risk that their new ideas and experiences will be perceived as threats and not as opportunities of innovation is considerable. We favour our own special interests rather than look at the interest of the company. This creates problems that will soon absorb any potential co-ordination gains.

Is this the whole truth? According to an international survey carried out by the management firm A.T. Kearney, 58 per cent of all mergers fail — for the Nordic countries the figure is 70 per cent! What would the alternative have been? When Volvo tried to take over Scania in August 1999, nobody knew whether the merger would succeed or not. But various infallible pundits immediately published quite contradictory analyses. When Volvo started acquiring Scania shares, various experts made the following statements.

"Scania has the ability to develop on its own ... We have lodged a demand that Volvo must get rid of its Scania stock."

Marcus Wallenberg, CEO of Investor, at Scania's annual general meeting in April 1999.

"Merging Volvo and Scania will weaken both companies and lead to the disappearance of thousands of jobs ... We shall lose market share if we merge. In terms of volume, we are talking about 30,000 vehicles long term. That corresponds to about 15,000 jobs and a drop in gross earnings of 0,75x to $1 billion. History shows that mergers of this kind generate nothing but costs and only have a very slim chance of succeeding."

Leif Östlig, CEO of Scania, on 3 May 1999.

This is not loose talk as far as Östlig is concerned, but a statement based on a feasability study backed by the entire group management and the board of directors.

When the merger was presented on 6 August 1999 he was sitting there, together with the Volvo and investor managements, defending the agreement. Had all his arguments only been shrewd negotiation tactics and tough rhetoric to pressurize Volvo into making a higher bid, or is the truth that there is no absolute truth? If you're facing the choice between two evils, you have to chose the lesser. A choice that you will then have to explain and justify by means of the arguments best suited to the occasion.

Who, then, among the parties turned out to be right? No one! Early in 2000 the EU disallowed the merger. On 27 March 2000, Volkswagen became a principal shareholder in Scania. Volvo had to find itself another partner. Does this mean that it is a better solution? All this speculation seems to be rather pointless. No-one can really know what the result would have been if the EU had approved Volvo's acquisition of Scania.

These decisions to merge are often made with little apparent consideration for the people who are chiefly affected — the employees. They must, as the saying goes, get out of the kitchen if they don't like the heat, and find themselves another job.

A.T. Kearney carried out a comprehensive analysis, and in the book *After the Merger*, they arrived at the conclusion that 86 per cent of all the companies investigated admit that their communication has not been good enough at the time of the merger negotiations. Communication is extremely important when the stakeholders of the company — employees as well as shareholders — are to be convinced of the new vision.

Communication or the post-merger period accounts for 53 per cent of the potential risk sphere, whereas negotiations account for 17 per cent, according to Kearney.

Another important discovery is that most mergers or partnerships that fail do so because the parties seek only to achieve internal savings and forget about potential added value.

> Most mergers or partnerships that fail do so because the parties seek only to achieve internal savings and forget about potential added value.

'Sykes survived Leschly's backhand,' read a headline in a leading European business paper on 19 January 2000 when the creation of the world's biggest pharmaceutical group was announced. The article continued as follows.

"The word is that it is a matter of billions of pounds, and they are creating the world's biggest group in pharmaceuticals, with a market value of $162 billion. But at the end of the day, what matters is how the two top people at the negotiating table get on with it — in this case in an elegant building in Chester Square at the centre of the exclusive Belgravia district in London just behind Buckingham Palace. The building is the corporate headquarters of SmithKline Beecham, one of the world's biggest pharmaceutical companies."

When the SmithKline/Glaxo merger was first attempted some years ago, it was shot down in flames, most likely as a result of disagreements between the Dane, Jan Leschly, CEO of SmithKline Beecham, and Sir Richard Sykes, chairman of the board in Glaxo. As the retirements of the two loomed nearer, which might have served to reduce rivalry between them, the merger came off. A question of human emotional factors exclusively.

The Economist wrote on 16 December 2000: 'Nowhere have malcontents been more evident in recent weeks than at Donaldson, Lufkin & Jenrette (DLJ). Since being acquired by Credit Suisse in September, DLJ's bankers have been rushing for the exits. On December 5th, Ken Moelis, who had turned DLJ into the leading junk-bond underwriter (so creating a big reason for the acquisition), became the latest high-profile departure. He and six colleagues are joining UBS. Another merger where all is not well is that between J.P. Morgan and Chase Manhattan. As the two firms combine operations, morale has plunged. There are concerns about the quality of Chase's loan portfolio and about job cuts to come.'

Some say that mergers and entering a new relation in business life is like second marriages, a triumph of hope over experience.

This book is about the human factor, and the ability to negotiate, not about the economic theories and analyses behind the mergers, or about who was right and who was wrong in their forecasts. How did various people react to, and during, the process shaping future co-operation? What happens in the course of negotiations? What are the reasons why few go well, and most do not? Can an alternative way of negotiating lead to more successes? Above all, personal chemistry matters just as much in mergers as it does in marriages. And it matters most at the top.

We are using the terms 'co-operation' and 'partnership' as synonymous with the process in which individuals attempt to act together to achieve a common objective, realize the added value, develop the undertaking, minimize harm and counteract threats. It is a process in which we all become involved, not just business executives, directors, or high-level political decision makers. It makes heavy demands on our ability to negotiate. This kind of co-operation in negotiations is becoming increasingly common and is essential for companies who wish to compete successfully.

When addressing the issue of realizing the added value, more than 80 per cent of your time should be devoted into really understanding the counterpart's business issues in the first place. This may be a tremendous investment that you can only afford to do as part of a deeper relationship.

Most co-operation projects are too insignificant to arouse the interest of the media. Tens of thousands of negotiations take place every day in this country. Individuals who have their backgrounds in different cultures and assumptions and abilities have to fit in with each other and work together to get an enormous bit of machinery to function. More and more we have to rely on other people to get our lives and daily doings to hang together. Technical developments make us dependent on people with specialist knowledge that we neither have nor have the time to acquire. Individuals are facing major demands. Demands creating stress and fear, turning them into a threat against the well-being of individuals. A human being under stress ceases to act as a rational being. Because of their number, these negotiations are more important than the large-scale mergers reflected by the big headlines.

The human factor

As early as in 1979 in our *Manual on Business Negotiations*, we discussed the importance of the human factor for the outcome of negotiations, and we warned against only basing business transactions and agreements on an exaggerated faith in technical and financial factors. Decisions are rarely rational and conscious. What is rational to one individual can be completely unintelligible to others. To many of the technicians, economists, and lawyers leaving our universities to carry out important assignments in business, industry, and administration, the human factor is an unknown concept.

Today universities are starting to realize that something is missing from many curricula. Researchers are beginning to examine what happens when attitudes, feelings and habits have to be merged. From the research project 'Management Across Borders', in which a group of researchers from the Gothenburg Business School studied Volvo's co-operation with Mitsubishi at Nedcar in the Netherlands, we know that transactions are often examined from a financial and organizational perspective, but that the human factor is forgotten. Ethnic background, corporate culture, and personality often play a more important role than people acknowledge.

Encountering problems in relation to the human factor is nothing new; we have witnessed this countless times during the 25 years we have been active in the field of negotiation. The methods for co-operation and partnership that we use as a basis for our courses originate in experience gleaned in thousands of different types of negotiations. We have charted the critical elements:

- how added value can be created;
- how added value can be divided;
- how successful negotiators differ from those who fail.

This book clarifies the mechanisms behind the human factor, the successes and the failures.

Partnership = co-operation

Two parties initiating or modifying some form of co-operation characterize a normal partnership. They are looking for long-term, stable relationships that will benefit them both. Some examples are provided below.

First party	Second party
Factory	Seeking a retail outlet for its products
Manufacturing company	Looking for an external property management firm to take care of the administration of its premises
Three construction companies	Join forces in a consortium in connection with a large-scale building project
Publishing house	Wishes to publish an encyclopaedia and is looking for authors/editors
Government	Wants to improve employment rates and promises subsidies
Telecoms operator	Wishes to launch new services

First party	Second party
Partner	Wants to change his involvement in a firm
Local authority	Wishes to put out for tender its social services to the elderly
Several departments in a company	Become involved in a joint project

In all the above cases, the hope is that partnership will yield a solution that is superior to the current ones. The aim is to reduce costs and risks, improve earnings and to take advantage of each other's experience and contacts.

Worldwide, billions of negotiations take place every day, and they are all aimed at getting all the details to fall into place. The people who meet have often 'been raised' in different corporate cultures, they have never negotiated with each other before, they see the negotiation from different angles, they have their own territories to guard, they don't want to lose the 1000 employees who will no longer be needed if rationalization can be achieved. Many of them are not accustomed to negotiating. Cultural clashes and infringements create suspicion and aggressiveness, which, in turn, lead many negotiators to perceive negotiations as a zero-sum game. What is worse is that in zero-sum games, no added value is created nor any agreement that works out in the longer term.

> Cultural clashes and infringements create suspicion and aggressiveness, which, in turn, lead many negotiators to perceive negotiations as a zero-sum game.

The human factor is one of the weightiest explanations why so many co-operation projects fail. The individuals involved do not function as rationally as the computers that can be employed to simulate its way to the best solutions. Human beings never have access to all the relevant information, and very often their decisions are widely based on emotions that may seem entirely alien to a third-party observer. Emotions are not part of rational calculations on which the partnership is based. Our experience is reinforced by the studies presented by *The Economist* and others concerning this problem in connection with mergers, big and small.

Why most attempts fail

Our experience in the majority of the partnership negotiations we have studied is depressing. A third of all negotiations fail entirely, parties who have good chances of achieving considerable added value, or to help each other reach their respective objectives, never manage to get any co-operation going; they part company without achieving anything. They are forced to choose an alternative that is decidedly less advantageous to them.

The other two-thirds do manage to reach an agreement, but 40 per cent of the potential added value and the objectives set for the negotiation fall by the wayside.

This shouldn't be viewed too negatively. For someone who masters the art of negotiating, there is a great untapped potential that we can all get a share of to improve our prosperity and well-being. Conflicts between seemingly incompatible objectives can suddenly be resolved when we have learned to listen to and respect each other. We must learn to take advantage of all the opportunities. You can really help yourself to what is on offer, you can achieve your objectives and get a bigger slice of the cake without having to make the other party feel that he is worse off. In this book we will show you how this feat can be accomplished.

> "... Partnering offers good potential to improve the value of money of construction. To be successful however, all parties — departments and the whole supply chain — must be fully committed to making the relationship work."
>
> National Audit Office Report January 2001

Management visions – employees' daily diet

The chief buyer in a large motor company is a visionary, who speaks of strategies for partnership buying. He states that he fully subscribes to the notion that partnership is advantageous. Reality for his supplier is completely different than the one outlined by the chief buyer in his strategy document. Many suppliers have tales to tell about the ever-harsher negotiation climate, growing risks, demands for bigger investments in combination with declining profits. Their perception is that they are exposed to combat rather than an invitation to join a partnership. The balance of power between the two parties is sometimes so biased that the party in whose favour the balance has tipped feels entitled to dictate terms.

To the buyer, negotiations that were originally seen as the start of long-term co-operation have turned into a game that he wants to win, because he wants to show that he has won, because at the negotiating table he has been able to squeeze his supplier into making considerable one-sided concessions. A game in which the welfare and well-being of many people may be at stake.

Some key problems areas – and solutions

Competent and incompetent negotiators

What distinguishes one from the other? In this chapter you will see how different kinds of human behaviour affect negotiations positively or negatively (without going too deeply into psychology). We describe different types of behaviours and give you our explanation of how an alternative behaviour could have yielded a better result.

Why co-operation yields superior solutions

We provide you with the explanation of why $2+2$ can equal 7. Real-life examples demonstrate to you how much added value it is possible to create. The aim of the chapter is to convince those who have not yet bought the gospel of partnership to open their eyes to its potential.

Only the negotiator who believes in co-operation will be motivated to go the whole hog.

This is where we look for added value

We focus on a number of factors that are often part of a deal, and we show you how, by trying out alternative methods, you can create added value and reduce costs and risks, or increase profits and other benefits. We try to show you that by viewing negotiations from a broader perspective than your usual one, you can locate new alternatives. The aim of the chapter is to provide you with new impulses to look for the added value, and with specific examples of what other undertakings and industries have done.

Not everything can be measured in terms of money or technical performance

Our decisions cannot exclusively be illustrated or motivated through financial or technical calculations in which we demonstrate concrete added value. There is a dimension beyond these, something that cannot be measured and is often difficult to comprehend for the people we are negotiating with and perhaps even for us. The aim of the chapter is to shed light on a negotiation from a different angle, and to engender better understanding of the factors that behave irrationally in the eyes of an outside observer.

How we can divide the added value located

Here the negotiator faces a dilemma, the openness required if we are to actually locate potential added value is not as obviously needed when the added value is to be divided. The division forces us into a zero-sum game, we have to change our approach. There is no list of correct results. The aim of the chapter is to show you the advantages, disadvantages and risks associated with the different approaches that work more or less well in different contexts.

What conditions must exist for co-operation to work?

Our experience shows that there are a number of fundamental factors that must necessarily be present if a partnership is to work, the human factor being one of them. The aim of the chapter is to draw attention to the fact that far from all business transactions, agreements and conflicts can be settled by means of a partnership.

Risks involved in co-operation

Co-operation and partnership are not cure-all solutions, which always guarantee a better outcome of negotiations than a traditional zero-sum game. There are certain risks that you must be aware of. Is your partner a co-operation-orientated one or is he a combative negotiator who is looking to exploit your openness?

2
Good and bad negotiators – what are the differences?

By studying a large group of negotiators to see whether there are significant differences between those who are successful and those who are not, we can form a clear picture of some of the factors which influence the negotiation result in a positive or negative direction. This also gives us a picture of why problems occur and how they can be avoided or handled. At the same time we must remember that this is not the answer to or the simple explanation of success or failure. Sometimes, the fundamental prerequisites are so bad that no negotiation technique can create any further success. Sometimes the prerequisites are so favourable that it is impossible to fail. Some negotiators are lucky while others simply run into bad luck.

One company manager told us that he only recruited lucky people. When we asked him how he found the lucky ones, he said:

> "We had been looking for a new sales manager and had received more than 100 applications from people who could document that they had the necessary qualifications. The first thing I did was to throw 90 of them into my wastepaper basket. The 10 which were not thrown out were lucky, and we hired one of them."

Over 1000 negotiators have been tested

The result is based on our studies of about 1000 negotiators who have gone through simulation negotiations of varying difficulty. They have included different types of partnerships: development projects, agency agreements, consortiums, annual agreements, joint ventures and co-operation across national borders within one organization. The negotiators who participated in the test were representatives of international business life. They came from companies within different sectors, of different sizes and with varying market positions. With respect to profession they were project managers, buyers, purchase managers, finance managers, IT managers, CEOs, sellers, sales managers and technical managers. In other words, those with daily responsibility for the business negotiations in their company. Most of them were well educated and had a basic academic education.

The exercises did not make special demands for technical, financial or trade-related knowledge. The prerequisites were formulated in such a way that it was absolutely possible to reach an agreement which was better than the alternatives presented. The decisive factor was their negotiation skill. The experiences gained in the study correspond very well with our experiences from similar real life negotiations.

How much do all the mistakes cost?

The studies show that only two-thirds of all negotiators land a deal, and then even one where they lose, on average, around 40 per cent of the overall negotiation potential. This potential consists of unutilized yet realizable added value which would have enabled the parties to get more out of the transaction without the opponent feeling like the loser. In this potential we will certainly find part of the added value which negotiators envisage when they calculate great merger gains. An added value which never will be realized now and which contributes to the failure of the majority of all major mergers.

The question of how much all the mistakes cost is impossible to answer. By looking at one single instance of negotiation, we will try to find out what the consequences are when negotiators fail in finding the most economical solution to the problem under negotiation.

In a negotiated agreement where the price is $1 million, the supplier has a gain of 25 per cent, which most people would consider a very nice gain. But when we look at all the data which is available to the parties, we can see that an added value of $200,000 in total could have been created. This added value can be realized if they design the agreement differently than originally planned for in the offer, e.g. by suggesting alternative payment conditions, another delivery time, a changed technical requirement specification and improved servicing.

During the negotiations they arrive at some of the changes which will provide the added value but if they negotiate as the average negotiator in our study did, as much as 40 per cent of the realizable added value of $200,000, i.e. $80,000, will remain unutilized. If it was the seller, e.g., who had found this $80,000 and he alone would benefit, his profit would have grown from $250,000 to $330,000, i.e. by as much as 32 per cent.

To this can be added that a little more than a third of the negotiators who participated in the test failed completely and never managed to enter into an agreement. The gain they lose is even greater. The overall cost of all the mistakes committed at the negotiation table will most likely amount to very large amounts. Added to this are the very negative effects in the shape of superfluous environmental destruction, a poor working environment, unnecessary technical and economic risks, and the time and energy the negotiators invest in fighting.

Even though the mistakes are very costly, we should not let the result depress us. Instead of focusing on the failures, we ought to look at the great potential available. For the skilled negotiator there is a lot to gain. The negotiation skill can and must be developed. Many companies are not so good at protecting and benefiting from their intellectual capital. The money and resources spent on developing the employees' negotiation skills are far too little compared to the enormous potential available.

The 'ketchup effect'

The study shows that during the 120 minutes which the negotiators have at their disposal, only about 10 per cent can finish without feeling any pressure of time. Over half (55 per cent) do not reach an agreement until the moment when they feel that time is running out. Under stress and pressed for time, they force a conclusion through. This can also be experienced in real life. When time is almost up, the negotiators are forced to reach an agreement, often in the shape of a compromise where the parties meet half way, i.e. no one must lose more than the other. Since there is no time to reconsider, they cannot be sure that all the significant points have been discussed and studied.

To study whether time had been lacking and whether this had influenced the result, the group of negotiators who had not reached an agreement after two hours was given another chance by having the negotiation period prolonged by another 30–60 minutes. In the group which had been given more time, only six per cent managed to reach an agreement. The others could not break their destructive pattern. A skilled observer of negotiations would have realized at an early stage that these negotiators would have a hard time. A description of the characteristics which usually manifest themselves will follow later in the chapter.

Time seems to have been of minor importance. Despite the extra time, a third of the negotiators failed to reach an agreement. Nothing came of the planned partnership about which they were supposed to reach an agreement.

Finished in good time	10% in total
Finished after two hours, a further 55%	65% in total
Finished after three hours, a further 2%	67% in total
Never finished	33% in total

The study shows that the small group of 10 per cent which managed to reach an agreement at their own pace, without getting stressed as a result of lack of time also entered into better agreements than the others. They utilized up to 20 per cent more of the available negotiation potential. They spent their time differently to those who found themselves pressed for time.

It is not lack of time which makes the negotiation fail. What causes the failure is the negotiation methods — a fact which many have difficulty accepting.

During the exercise we tried to step in and help the negotiators who had got stuck in meaningless arguments and those who had reached a dead end, having come up with solutions that were unacceptable for various reasons. This kind of assistance is not available in real negotiations of course.

In around 10 per cent of the negotiations which let to a conclusion, one of the parties declared: 'If this had been a real negotiation situation, we would have stopped a long time ago and thrown the opponents out. We would never have accepted their behaviour. But since this is an exercise, we wanted to give them a chance'.

The significance of this is that there is a considerable risk that the negotiators would have been even less successful in real negotiations. It is at the negotiation table that your company can win or lose great sums of money in a short time.

How to get a bigger slice of the cake

In our studies we found great variations in the behaviour at the negotiation table, but there is a significant behaviour which recurs among many of the negotiators.

It is not lack of time which makes the negotiation fail. What causes the failure is the negotiation methods — a fact which many have difficulty accepting.

Key factors in successful negotiation

The following factors are common among the majority of those who do better than average in negotiations.

- They have analyzed the negotiation and the negotiation variables. They have prioritized important and less important variables.
- They have made a decision and put a price on the soft — and often immeasurable variables.
- They often outline the negotiation on a board to get an overview.
- They have incorporated the message of added value.
- They have the initiative during the negotiations.
- They are good at communicating.
- They have a high but realistic goal.
- They quickly start negotiating.
- They try to avoid problems by suggesting alternative solutions.
- They work actively on creating a positive negotiation climate.
- They actively present offers and counter offers.
- They have distributed the roles within the group and they are disciplined.
- They have a strategy.

- They work methodically.
- They do not dig foxholes and fight about details.
- They start bargaining in good time.
- They take one last break before entering into an agreement.
- They make a point of behaving in a credible manner.

Each of these factors is discussed in more detail below.

They have analyzed the negotiation and the negotiation variables

During that preparation, successful negotiations will have analyzed the negotiations and worked out a list of the likely negotiation variables, i.e. all the points that may be discussed. They know their own scope for negotiation in all these areas, and they know what they win or lose if the conditions are changed in one way or another. They have a good grasp of economics, and they can picture 'the deal'. They know how to double the money on one point by assuming a greater cost or risk on another. They have prioritized the variables. They demonstrate great firmness in the areas which are of great importance to the result. They signal willingness to compromise in the areas which are of less importance. They look at the overall result rather than the individual parts.

They have made a decision and put a price on the soft variables

They are aware that a number of 'soft' variables exist in negotiations which cannot be measured with the usual economic or technical goals. They have decided what they are willing to give and forgo in order to:

- keep a regular customer;
- avoid the insecurity of waiting and instead reach an agreement today;
- live on the fourth floor instead of the first;
- move into a house where they feel happy people live;
- co-operate with people who treat them with respect and as an equal partner;
- avoid dealing with negotiators who fight.

They often outline the negotiation on a board to get an overview

During their preparations, they often outline the negotiation on a board to get an overview. This picture helps them to see which parts of the negotiation are connected, e.g. how a demand for shorter delivery times can be matched with a demand for a big advance payment — an advance which is worth more to the supplier than the possible cost of forcing the production. This will be very helpful when they start bargaining.

Often they contrast the different alternatives to help them get an overview of the different scenarios. This way they are better prepared if the negotiations should take an unexpected turn. This ability to analyze is especially prominent among people who end up in business life after a career in the armed services.

They have incorporated the message of added value

They have incorporated the message of added value. They know that by means of luck and skills they can reach a solution which is more attractive than their opening offer.

They are motivated to co-operate. It is clear to them how the added value can arise, and where they should look for it. They make use of this skill in their preparations when they are setting up a list of the possible negotiation variables.

They have the initiative during the negotiations

They have the initiative during the negotiations. They have understood that the initiator has an information reserve which is to his advantage when the added value is to be distributed.

The initiative does not lie with the person who speaks and argues very much. It lies with the party who is in control of the situation by asking questions, listening and following up with summaries and consequence questions.

They find out which variables are negotiable and whether changes of the conditions may entail added value. They provide themselves with a clear picture of the size of the added value which may be created. They are skilled at procuring information. For example, if they suspect that the opponent can benefit from a shorter delivery time, they are not so naive that they think they can get an answer to the question 'How much could you make if we shortened the delivery time by one month?' They choose another way.

- They open a discussion about some other point in the negotiation, e.g. how much the daily penalty fine would amount to in case of delays in delivery. They ask what the customer thinks is fair and why. It is a fair assumption that the value of a shorter delivery time to some extent equals what a delay would cost. Their counter offer could be: 'If we accept day fines of the size you demand, are you then prepared to give us a bonus of a similar amount if we can deliver earlier?'

- They initiate a discussion with the customer about whether he can accept to grant them a longer delivery deadline. If not, they would like to know why and what consequences there would be of an extension to the deadline. Then they move on to the discussion of an agreed penalty.

- They offer the customer two alternatives: a small price reduction or using the resources on reducing the delivery time instead. The customer chooses the alternative which suits him the best, and in this way he has accepted that a reduction of the delivery time is valuable.

They do not accept a 'no'. You can get around some obstacles if you know why the customer said no. Instead of arguing, they spend more time on mapping out the negotiation possibilities.

They are good at communicating

They have a highly developed communicative competence. Their presentation is characterized by self confidence and enthusiasm, and they are good at giving presentations and illustrating advantages to the opponent by means of different alternatives. They are good at listening and have a well-developed question technique.

They have high but realistic goals

They have more ambitious goals than keeping within budget or reaching an agreement which is a little bit better than the next best alternative. At times they put off specifying their goal until they have got to know the opponent better and received a better impression of the parties' mutual relative strengths.

They clearly communicate their goals, which influences the opponent's level of ambition. They have a realistic picture of where the line is between an insultingly low offer and a high offer. They can support their demands by credible arguments. They adjust their goal if new information provides them with a new picture of possibilities and limitations.

They quickly start negotiating

They quickly start negotiating by limiting the time spent on arguing and instead concentrating on mapping out the possibilities. They have the courage to open up and make a certain amount of information available, while those who fail fight shy of it. They realize that if you want something, you have to be willing to give something yourself. Because they dare take the first step and be open, the opponent lets his guard down and mirrors their behaviour.

They do not spend much time on arguing in the beginning. It is not until they have formed a better picture of the opponent's priorities and what the different changes of conditions mean to the opponent that they spend more time arguing. They use the arguments to support their offer, and explain why their offer is to the advantage of the opponent.

They try to avoid problems by suggesting alternative solutions

When they run into problems, they often try to get around them by suggesting alternative solutions. They rarely get stuck in meaningless arguments about whose proposition or perception of the facts is true or false.

This method has been called the 'sun and wind' method after Aesop's fable. If the wind tries to blow the coat of a man, he will only hold it even tighter. If the sun warms him, he will willingly take it off. Because they do not try to use force, threats, power or sharp rhetoric in order to force the opponent down on his knees, they largely avoid pinning themselves down on prestige questions. They do not make the mistake of insulting the opponent.

They will often express themselves in terms such as 'That was an interesting proposal, but how do you propose to arrange financing?' Let us call it the 'yes, but' principle.

They create a positive negotiation climate

They create a positive negotiation climate, characterized by mutual respect. They have a good understanding and feeling of the human factor and seem to realize that pressure breeds counter pressure and that insults cause strong emotional reactions. They treat the opponent as an equal partner and avoid expressions such as 'You are just subcontractors', 'You only handle the administrative work,' 'Everybody can presumably provide reception personnel', 'You ought to realize that we do not have time for that sort of thing'.

They listen to the opponent and summarize the picture they have formed of his views and thus gain his respect and trust. They do not mix this with a subservient attitude but are very aware of the necessity of standing by their own demands. They are gentle on the outside but tough on the inside.

They are easy to get along with and they spend time talking about the weather and showing a genuine interest in the other party. Their social skills are good. In order to get to know the opponent better and to gain his trust, they search for common interests beside the things they negotiate about.

They actively present offers and counter offers

They are not only goal-oriented people who take the initiative. They also actively present offers and counter offers. Where others are hampered, unable to make a decision and avoid conflicts, they bargain. They have learned the rules of give and take. All types of one-sided concessions are avoided. Instead of just accepting the first offer within their budget, they dare to continue.

They seem to be aware that the person who dares present the first offer also determines the frame of reference for the continuous negotiation. If the opponent is the first to present an offer which deviates from what they themselves had in mind, they reject the opponent's offer. They do not want this to be the basis of the continuous negotiations. Instead of counter arguing and attempting to adjust the opponent's offer, they react with their own counter offer.

They have a strategy

They have a general plan — a strategy for the negotiation — and therefore they are ready to keep the initiative. They push the negotiation ahead. They are selfconfident and do not get stuck. Examples of different strategies can be found in Appendix 2.

They know that they have to change their method during the negotiations and become significantly tougher when they approach the question of the distribution of costs, risks and gains. They see no conflict in having to shift to a zero-sum game and can therefore keep the initiative throughout the negotiations.

They have distributed the roles within the group and they are disciplined

During the preparations they have spent time discussing the group's working method. They have divided the roles among themselves. They have a negotiation leader who speaks for the group. Another person in the group listens and observes the game and keeps his colleagues informed about what is really going on. A third does calculations and keeps track of how the change of conditions being discussed will affect the overall result. They are disciplined, and leave it up to the negotiation leader to conduct the negotiations. Spontaneous ideas, obstructing each other or presenting double messages rarely happen. If the negotiation leader gets into trouble, one of the others steps in and suggests that they have a break. Prior to crucial negotiations they take a break so that the negotiation leader can consult the group.

They have agreed on how the group's internal communication is to be handled. Sign language, eye contact, small written notes and breaks are among the techniques they employ.

They work methodically

They are structured and methodical. It is normal to have agendas. They use flip charts and boards for joint note taking and summaries. They do not leap back and forward between the individual points but negotiate about every single question until there is nothing more to discuss. Before they go from one point to the next, they sum up to make sure that they have understood each other correctly.

They do not dig themselves in foxholes and fight about details

Instead of becoming immersed in details, they focus the negotiations on the important points. If they can agree on these, the other things will come into place. The details can be handled by the people directly affected by them.

They avoid verbal fights about details. They agree with the other party and give in to the opponent's demands on the less important points. But the giving in is not one-sided. All concessions are used to obtain improvements on the points which are important to them. They are aware that concessions which do not cost them anything can be of significant value to the opponent. They demand to get their share when they make a concession.

They start bargaining in good time

They are determined not to waste any time. To argue and counter argue leads to meaningless 'trench warfare' and provides only limited information about the available possibilities. If they encounter an opponent who does not want to answer questions, they quickly move on with another method; they present an offer. The opponent makes up his mind one way or another about the new offer, and in this way, important information is given.

Because they start bargaining early, they have time for two or three breaks during this phase where they can evaluate, at their own leisure, how the negotiations are going.

They take one last break before entering into an agreement

They do not allow themselves to be stressed into making a decision at the table in the cases where the opponent presents a so-called 'final' offer. Even though the offer is good and within the goal they have set up, they take one last break to check, at their own leisure, whether they have exhausted all possibilities and landed a good and profitable agreement. They take one last discussion within the group about the appropriateness of testing the limits one more time. In real life, this break may take a day or two.

They make a point of behaving in a credible manner

They acknowledge the importance of being perceived as credible by the opponent. They stick to the truth and do not invent arguments. They do not send double messages. They are true to their word and avoid tactical moves aimed at creating insecurity.

Reasons for failure

When negotiations fail, the group's behaviour varies a lot but in every failing negotiation a number of the errors below can be found.

- They only see half the negotiation.
- They aim too low.
- They do not actively search for the added value.
- They throw themselves into traditional negotiation fights.
- The price is more important than the overall costs.
- The concept of added value is vague to them.
- They overlook the totality.
- They do not realize that the partner also has to make money.
- They are afraid of opening up.
- They work in an unstructured manner.
- They have not distributed the roles within the group.
- They are afraid of bargaining.
- They do not set up a strategy.
- They lose the grip on the economics.
- They make insultingly low offers.
- They do not accept that the opponent has to make money.
- They seek 'fair' solutions.
- They are not good at listening.

Each of these factors is discussed in more detail below.

They only see half the negotiation

Poor negotiators only see their side of the negotiations, i.e. what they get and give, and they have no feeling whether the change of conditions which they force will provide any added value or instead contribute to an unnecessarily expensive agreement. Nor can they see how gains in one area, e.g. a lower price, will be eaten up by additional costs and increased risks in another., e.g. maintenance costs which lie under another budget or affect another person's budget.

They are occupied with guarding their own preserves and have not understood the point of partnership — that they face a project with the purpose of reducing the overall costs and risks and increasing the joint earnings of both parties.

The politicians' behaviour in connection with the Telia/Telenor merger showed that they were not capable of or interested in negotiating with a view to achieving the best solution for the new company. Instead, national special interests resulted in never-ending disagreement about services, locations, titles, salaries and other details. We were shown an egoism controlled by the involved actors' own political purposes which lowered the expected value of a merged Telia/Telenor by several billion Swedish Kroner. Finally, the entire deal fell apart at the finishing line and the parties now negotiate about sharing the bill for its failure.

A buyer can make demands for an earlier delivery date. This may be practical for the buyer. The economic value is limited to $10,000, but another supplier has offered to deliver earlier without any extra cost for the buyer. He demands that the supplier with whom he is negotiating now accepts the same demand and guarantees a shorter delivery time. If the supplier tries to get paid for this by saying: 'That will be more expensive for us', the customer will flatly refuse the demand by referring to the conditions offered by the competitor. The supplier caves in and accepts the customer's demand although the reduction of the delivery time will cost him $50,000. The concession does not lie within his negotiation scope which is there to cover costs of any new demands. With the knowledge of both parties' prerequisites, we can show that the buyer has needlessly made the transaction $40,000 more expensive.

If the seller is not open and plays with his cards on the table and explains that this will cost him $50,000, the buyer cannot know how cost and risk increasing his demand is. The customer only looks at the effects which a change of conditions has on him and not at how it will affect the economy and risks of others.

When you ask the people who negotiate this way why they are afraid of dialogue and openness, they answer: 'The opponent can take care of himself. It cannot be our job to attend to the opponent's interests. If they do not react and make counter offers, why encourage them by asking questions?'.

If the customer can negotiate a concession to the value of $10,000 without having to give anything in return, his one-track mindedness makes him believe that he has got this 10,000 for free and made a good effort. What is free for him is not free for the opponent.

In order not to fall into the trap, they should have done as follows.

They have should learned to prepare themselves in another way and also to see the negotiation from the opponent's point of view. A useful tool for them may be the timetables in Appendix 1.

When discussing change of conditions, the negotiators must actively search for information or ask questions: 'How does this affect you? If we do it this or that way instead, how will it affect you?'

They need insight into the difference between a zero-sum game and a partnership. They have to understand that nothing is free. There is always a price to pay for their 'success' even though the price is invisible to them. Wrong decisions can only be avoided if they know how both parties are affected. They have to ask more questions before making decisions: 'If we were prepared to forgo our demand for quicker delivery and leave things the way they were, what would you do about the price in return?' This presupposes dialogue, a communication skill that inexperienced negotiators do not master. They may even be afraid of it.

Some negotiators use the method of returning to the original proposition as a conscious tactic. First, the buyer negotiates a number of changes which he really does not benefit from. By threatening his opponent that nothing will come of the deal, he forces him to accept his demands. He listens to and makes note of the objections which the seller has. He is very particular about writing all the costs down and does not object to their size. At the end of the negotiation the buyer suddenly changes his mind. Now he wants the original terms to apply but the counter claim is a price reduction. The buyer then uses the seller's own arguments to demand a price reduction of the same size as the extra cost and risk which the seller mentioned earlier.

A great part of the responsibility falls on the managers if they do not teach their negotiators to look at the totality. The administrative routines and calculation methods of the company may need to be re-evaluated so that they do not encourage so-called sub-optimizing, where a cost saved in one area becomes eaten up by significant extra costs which affect other departments or another budget year. Traditional ways of thinking and the 'us and them' mentality must be overcome.

If the fight strategy gets in the way, companies ought to consider whether this is the correct strategy to use in the future.

They aim too low

Poor negotiators start out by aiming too low and not leaving room for negotiation, instead of having an open mind about what the best possible deal may look like. Their goal is to keep within budget or to reach an offer which is somewhat better than their second-best alternative. This mistake is especially common among buyers. There are even buyers who will give the deal to the supplier who has offered the lowest price without having negotiated with the others.

After having zeroed the received offers, a buyer can face three alternatives:

> A with an overall cost of 1.1 million
> B with an overall cost of 1.175 million
> C with an overall cost of 1.31 million

From the above, C is immediately rejected. Since his overall cost is so high compared to the others, his offer can be judged as uninteresting. What C might have done if the parties had sat down to look at the possible alternatives, will never be investigated. Could C have misunderstood the buyer's wishes? No one knows.

Negotiations have been carried out with A which ended with A declaring that he had already made his best offer. Now B should be given the chance of making a better offer than A. A lot of these buyers have the attitude: 'We already have a supplier who can cover our needs and who has made an acceptable offer. His technical solution is completely satisfactory. We do not have to make an effort; it is the other supplier who has to improve his offer if he is going to stand a chance.'

With this attitude, the buyer is not especially motivated to actively search for the added value himself. You can tell by some people's body language. They sit with their arms crossed. They are somewhat sullen, reserved, dismissive and unwilling to enter into a dialogue.

If B can match A's overall costs and end at less than 1.1 million he will get the deal the very moment he crosses the 'magic line'. That is what it takes.

In order not to fall into the trap, they should have done as follows.

When B had passed the 'magic line', they should have taken a break to evaluate the negotiation. A 10–15 minute postponement may prove worthwhile. If you have spent several days, perhaps even weeks, negotiating, you will also have time to spend a few extra minutes in the decisive moments.

During the negotiations the buyer has probably received more information about how supplier B views the deal, and they ought to ask themselves some questions:

- Are there other types of added value than the ones we have found? Have we looked at all the negotiable variables?

- What does the seller's calculation look like? Has he caved in at all and lowered his own margin or is the reduced overall cost which we have reached exclusively a result of the created added value? If yes, how has the added value achieved been distributed? Could it even be that the seller has not caved in at all but instead increased his profit? Should we then accept this?

- Should we enter into an agreement or continue to negotiate?

- Should we then accept the offer as it is? If there is to be a point in continuing to negotiate, the energy and time spent must be reasonable compared to the expected gains. If your analysis leads you to the conclusion that the seller also has had to reduce his own gain in order to push the overall cost down, there is only a slight chance that further negotiation will be worthwhile.

- A satisfied opponent has greater interest in and possibility of keeping his promises than a dissatisfied party who has been forced to forego any gain. Do not forget that the negotiations have not been concluded because the agreement has been entered into. The one who has been pressured to take on too much may face serious and expensive problems in the end phase.

- Should we ask for a new offer? If your analysis shows that the seller has created several types of added value and distributed these in such a way that he has improved his own gain while putting pressure on your overall costs, further negotiations may be worthwhile.

- Should we make a counter offer? This is reasonable if you want to test the opponent one last time, or if you are under so much time pressure that it is important to enter into an agreement quickly.

- Should we have a new negotiation round with the other suppliers? This is tempting because many of the propositions made by B have significant differences compared to the propositions made earlier by A. What is now being done in another way has created added value but you do not know to what extent A can offer the same or better conditions.

The question furthermore contains an ethical dimension: is it morally defensible to take B's ideas about alternative solutions and pass them on to the competitor A? Is this not theft of know-how? How will it affect your image as a buyer if rumours got started that you had behaved in this way? Is the price you would have to pay for such behaviour reasonably proportional to the negotiation gain which you can achieve by this single deal?

> They do not actively search for
> the added value

Poor negotiators are passive and let the opponent control the negotiations. They rarely have all the necessary information to find out where to create the possible added value. Maybe they have no insight into what partnership is. If the person is also an inexperienced negotiator, the parties will glide into the traditional zero-sum game. They have no knowledge of which variables are negotiable. They can only reach an agreement if one of the parties makes concessions.

If they are not active and investigate how the negotiable changes may be utilized to create added value, they leave the initiative with the opponent. If he is an experienced negotiator, he can create one type of added value after the other and keep the gain for himself. See Appendix 2.

In order not to fall into the trap, they should have done as follows.

They should have had the courage to be active, take the initiative and be in control of the negotiation by asking questions. Many need to have their communicative competence strengthened. They should learn to carry on an analytical dialogue. The opponent's demands should have been met with questions instead of accommodating or one-sided concessions. The person who cannot beat his passivity becomes an expensive negotiator, a negotiator no company can afford in the long run.

Everybody around the negotiation table is responsible for the negotiations. Thorough preparations and training can help a lot. It may be necessary to strengthen the negotiation delegation. If that does not help, the negotiators must be exchanged.

They throw themselves into traditional negotiation fights

Despite Norwegians' and Swedes' documented fear of conflicts, many Scandinavians *do* make use of traditional negotiation fights with a lot of arguing. To argue seems to be the only model they know. They have spent their energy and preparation time on finding good arguments. The opponent then has to accept them. The more and the better arguments the group can come up with, the more they believe that they are right.

The risk of unprofessionalism and bluff is great. We are attentive to such risks and warn the negotiators whose preparation work we follow, against beginning to believe in their own arguments. Our experience tells us that they risk finding themselves in a corner with no way out. They lack the ability of recognizing that they were wrong. Their prestige takes over the course of events.

Their communication is one-way, and there is a lack of questioning and active listening. They are always trying to squeeze the opponent as much as possible. The negotiators neither can nor dare be open. They are bad at coaxing information out of the opponent. When they cannot find new pieces to the puzzle which will provide a better picture of the negotiation possibilities, they get increasingly insecure and do not find the openings which can create added value. Their negotiations are characterized by lack of information. The access to relevant and new information is important if negotiators are going to create added value. What is missing is openness as well as the active search for information.

Negotiators who dare be open and direct in case of a conflict will not face problems with a lack of information or the frustration which takes hold of them when they do not make any progress.

In order not to fall into the trap, they should have done as follows.

They should have had the courage to accept the message of added value and to see what it might give. They must learn to get a dialogue going and discover that two-way communication is not dangerous. They have to break with the macho culture and its aggressiveness which characterize certain trades. It is deeply depressing to meet those 'tough guys' who say: 'Dialogue, that is a woman's thing. Real men make demands and give orders'.

They ought to create an overall picture for themselves of the important negotiations points, the information they themselves have, the additional information they ought to procure, and the information which they believe the opponent can benefit from in order to find new value adding alternatives. This is where the timetables come in (see Appendix 1).

The managers in the company have a big responsibility for creating change. It is not enough simply to declare a new policy or send out a memo with the title *Supplier co-operation — our strategy for the 21st century*. It is not just about getting the employees to buy the new strategy in theory. A lot of energy has to be put into training the employees in the method and getting them away from the deeply rooted fighting method.

The price is more important than the overall costs

Poor negotiators have an inadequate understanding of the overall costs or income within a project. They fail to see the deal. The price they have to pay is more important than the overall cost or the overall return. The negotiators have a diffuse perception of which elements should form part of the overall picture. Often they have not analyzed the negotiation variables, set them up and discussed conceivable changes and how they affect the result. The overall result cannot be found by means of the company's internal studies. Costs and gains are booked in different departments, on different accounts and in different budget years, which makes negotiators focus on the price.

For example, the choice is between two suppliers who offer an identical product. One of them demands $40 per unit and the other $41. Everybody can see that $40 is less than $41. This is money which must be taken from a purchase budget. The supplier who wants $40 demands an advance payment, whereas the competitor does not. In many companies, interest expenses are debited from another account, and many negotiators do not know how to calculate the interest and add it to the price of $40 to be able to compare the two offers.

Do not think that this is limited to small companies. At the negotiation courses we have held for a couple of the biggest Nordic listed companies — they are on the list of the 16 biggest companies in Scandinavia — the purchase managers said the following:

> "We do not care about the calculations; we have no information about which calculation factor to use and there are probably not many who can calculate the interest effect."

> "If money has been allocated in the budget, we do not have to deal with the interest as long as we spend the money within the same year."

> "We have developed our purchase method and established a new policy. As of new year we will not only look at the price but also at the overall costs."

In accordance with EU rules on public tendering, there are two criteria for the choice of supplier: lowest price or the one who has made the most favourable offer. To make things easy, many buyers make their choice based on the lowest price. If the selection criterion is price, the buyer must have specified and fixed all demands and prerequisites in his tender documents. These demands and prerequisites are non-negotiable. Once the tender has been made public, negotiations, especially price negotiations, with different suppliers are no longer allowed. Only vague points in the tender material may be discussed. It is self-evident that it is difficult to create added value with such a set of rules.

If the buyer instead chooses to use the most favourable offer as selection criterion, he is entitled to consider price and a number of predefined factors which affect the overall cost. It must appear in the buyer's tender material whether the selection criterion is price or overall costs.

In order not to fall into the trap, they should have done as follows.

The companies which suffer from incompetence or which encourage or make sub-optimizing possible should revise their accounting systems. They should do something about the preserves attitude so that both costs, risks and gains are included in the project and do not burden or reward the wrong people. The companies should learn to view the overall cost over the entire project's or the system's life cycle.

The managers in the company have a big responsibility for creating change. A lot has to be done in order to create an understanding of the life cycle and overall cost concepts.

The negotiations and the results ought to be documented to know which factors can be included in the decision and how they are measured. When the project has been completed, a calculation can be made which should be compared to the basis for decision to find out to what extent the right decisions were made. Knowing that a follow-up will take place, the individual negotiator may be motivated to enter on a new course. Like accounts, negotiations also ought to be revised.

The concept of added value is vague to them

To many negotiators, the concept of added value is vague. They do not realize that a measure which costs money can generate multiple returns, e.g. in the shape of costs saved, longer life or reduced risks.

Swedish skier Ingmar Stenmark said '*You can only talk with those who understand*'. Many negotiators lack economic as well as technical and practical knowledge of the things they negotiate about. They lack the ability to think in a business oriented manner.

Another group of negotiators hold their own against change. They are responsible for a company where they once worked out a solution which worked and has been working satisfactorily over the years. If someone then suggests that everything or something can be done in a different way, they see it as an invasion of their domain, as criticism of their work effort. Their experience and competence are being questioned. To these people negotiating is not about creating added value; it is about defending themselves against an invading enemy.

In order not to fall into the trap, they should have done as follows.

In the companies where competence is lacking or where preserves are guarded, this is a job for management. Training is not always enough. Not everybody can be trained to become good negotiators. Some people have to have other job assignments. Negotiation and project groups need to supplement their competence.

They overlook the totality

Individual details become far too important. Often negotiators get stuck on questions of details which neither have to do with very much money nor big risks, but everybody wants to express and assert their personal perception. There is no discipline in the group, and its single members easily find themselves in verbal fights with the opponent.

One reason for this is the lack of knowledge, another the fear of openness and conflicts, a third is insufficient preparation. The negotiators have not set up any priority, so all details seem to be of equally great importance to them. They theorize about every single little detail. Everybody wants to present their view. Nobody listens to the others.

Prestige takes over. In public and in the mass media the Swedish-Norwegian owners and negotiators in the Telia/Telenor merger start to argue whether it is fair that the new chairman of the board receives a salary of $625,000. Arguments like: 'Nobody is worth that salary. It is ten times as much as the Norwegian prime minister gets', are presented. No wonder that the stock-exchange analysts lower their assessment of the new group when they see that the owners spend all their energy fighting about details instead of considering how the company can be developed.

This is a problem which we have seen happen to Norwegian negotiators significantly more than to their Swedish counterparts. A Norwegian characteristic? When Finland, Norway and Sweden negotiated with the EU, the European negotiators were asked to paint a picture of their Nordic counterparts.

There was a lot of good to be said about the Finns. They were tough and goal-oriented with respect to the questions which were of vital importance to them. They had decided to enter the EU and to be whole-hearted Europeans.

It was difficult to negotiate with the Swedes, who often backed out of agreements already entered into. The decisions made at the negotiation table were apparently poorly rooted or ill-considered.

The Europeans never knew where they had the Norwegians. They made a fuss about everything. There did not seem to be any difference between trivial and important questions, which made it hard to figure out what the Norwegians really wanted.

Technicians make up another group where many need to place all the little pieces of the puzzle in their right place and in the right way. They seem less concerned about the totality. Many of them have a preference for theorizing instead of looking at how things can function in reality.

Focusing on irrelevant details is often described as 'bicycle stand syndrome'. Everybody has an opinion and prepared to express it on where to place the bicycle stand, but when it comes to the question of how to finance a million-dollar investment, there are not many who can and dare express their opinion.

Sometimes the strategy is to begin with less important questions in order to get to know the opponent and in order to build up a positive relationship. The less important questions appear to be more difficult than predicted. The perception of what is right and wrong can often be different. The negotiators get stuck before they reach the important issues. They experience that they are too far apart for further negotiations to be meaningful. We have often heard: 'If we cannot even agree on these less important details, there is no reason to continue'. If they had had a better grasp of the overall picture, the minor details which they disagree about may have been less important.

When negotiating, they compare price with price, payment conditions with payment conditions and warranty terms with warranty terms. For each point they seek solutions which are better than the one they have been offered by someone else. Because they isolate the negotiation variables, they may get a completely unrealistic perception of what they can achieve. They do not take into consideration that an opponent who has chosen to be generous on one point will take back what he has given on another point.

In order not to fall into the trap, they should have done as follows.

In their preparations they should have formed a clear picture of which factors are important. They can find help in the timetables in Appendix 1. They should have a clear negotiation goal and set up an agenda which would lead them towards the goal and which sort out irrelevant questions.

The negotiation leader has to have the strengths to cut in to suggest that the question be dealt with at a later stage or that the questions of details be solved by a couple of the assessors who are not directly involved in the negotiation. In the group there ought to be an observer who has the courage to signal his boss: 'Let us take a short break now, we are stuck'. The negotiators have to get rid of their reluctance to confront problems and must have the courage to take the bull by the horns.

They lack the understanding that the partner also has to make money

Poor negotiators cannot find the right balance between being businesslike and being miserly. They have a hard time accepting that a partner is entitled to make money on his project effort. These negotiators would like to see or have already calculated the opponent's costs or risks. Based on that they decide what the opponent is allowed to make. Instead of looking at what the opponent can give them in the shape of rationalizations and improved gains, they feel that they have the right to control that the opponent does not make too much.

We end up with a negotiation where the parties presuppose different realities. One of them wants to buy time at a reasonable cost per hour, and the other wants to sell his experience and be paid in accordance with the useful effect he can supply to the customer. The group of buyers who cannot accept this calls it market pricing. They can only accept a price which has been fixed in relation to the opponent's costs. The principle becomes more important than the problem they have to solve.

If you claim to have this right over others because of your own position of power or own value norms — a right based on a higher moral — you may shoot down a lot of potential co-operation projects. One of the most used arguments relates to fairness or justice. 'It is not fair to share a gain 30/70.' 'It is not fair that you make $900 an hour, while I make $400.'

In order not to fall into the trap, they should have done as follows.

It is important that we learn that value conflicts of this kind are very difficult to solve. Because the stand points are incompatible, it will also be difficult to find compromises that work.

In most negotiation situations we try to reach a competent agreement and one which is better than the alternatives we have and which does not offend our value norms. What gives us the right to claim that our value norms are better or more relevant than the opponent's? We have to be able to set our private value norms aside. Reality forces us to be practical and realize that co-operation agreements can work just fine even though we do not agree on the basic value norms on which a supplier's price is based. Realize that the one who earns himself a good profit is significantly more motivated to make good project efforts than the one who feels like a loser.

When evaluating whether a proposition is acceptable or not, we must compare it with our second-best alternative. More often than not justice has not so much to do with businesslike thinking as to allow it to prevent a deal.

They are afraid of opening up

Many negotiators make use of a strategy aimed at being able to wait longer than the opponent. This strategy is often rooted in the fact that the negotiators are poorly prepared. They are afraid to say too much, to reveal their positions and give the opponent the upper hand in the further negotiations. This strategy can be necessary if you have a poor knowledge of which problems and possibilities the negotiations present. It can also lead to a good result if the opponent is impatient and eager to close the deal.

The negotiations will suffer from lack of energy and fuel if new information does not present itself. You do not seem to be getting anywhere. Some give up prematurely and do not have the necessary energy to make an effort to find or offer openings. In the beginning the negotiators' problem is not that they lack time but that they have too few of the pieces of the puzzle to work with. When one of the parties then finally opens up, they find themselves lacking time. They have to rush the agreement through without the necessary time for thought and discussion. See The 'ketchup effect' earlier in this chapter.

The problems become clear if the opponent has chosen the same strategy. The parties circle each other, waiting for the other to open up. When this is not the case, two things may happen: Either the entire matter comes to nothing and you part without having started the real negotiations, or someone starts to argue about a harmless question of detail and the negotiations get stuck.

In order not to fall into the trap, they should have done as follows.

Negotiating is about giving and taking. If you want something, you must also be prepared to give something in return. If you want information, what kind of information can you give the opponent in return? One of the parties has to have the courage to take the first step and open up. You have to consider this in your preparations. Where can you open up and how much? Openness can never be complete, and the negotiator who puts all his cards on the table is naive.

For example, if you can make $10,000 by getting a delivery one month earlier, you have to consider how to present this.

- Wait and see whether the opponent raises the issue.

- Include the point as a general point on the agenda where you harmonize certain prerequisites of the agreement. '*Good, if we move on to the next point of the agreement, the delivery time, it reads 15 November in the offer. Do you have any comments on that?*'

- Refer to competitors: *'One of your competitors asked whether we would be interested in earlier delivery. This is something which could be of interest.'*

- Send a clear signal: *'You are more expensive but if we can have this delivered one month earlier, it will partly make up for the somewhat higher price.'*

- Make an offer: *'If you can deliver one month earlier, we will get a small profit which we can share with you. You will receive a bonus of $2,000.'*

They work in an unstructured matter

Poor negotiators work unstructured without an agenda. They do not use joint notes on the board or summaries. They leap back and forward between the individual points. Double messages can also be found. Insecurity, lack of preparation, poor discipline and an under-developed negotiation technique are some of the explanations. It becomes a hotchpotch of a negotiation where nobody sees the deal and the existing possibilities. The opponent becomes unsure of the negotiator's intentions.

In order not to fall into the trap, they should have done as follows.

They should spent more time preparing, and they should have learned to work with an agenda. They should have got used to always summing up before they moving from one discussion point to the next and taking joint notes on the board. There should be many breaks with the purpose of establishing within the group whether they are on the right track and agreeing on a joint attitude internally in the negotiation delegations.

This way of co-operating can seem stiff and formal to many people, but the discipline must be incorporated before you can let go and improvize without entirely losing control of the negotiation.

They have not distributed the roles within the group

Poor negotiators do not distribute the roles within the group, and they are undisciplined. The group members present different messages, and they risk beginning to negotiate with and reprimand each other in front of the opponent. They make decisions about questions where they have some technical knowledge but not about how the overall business is affected.

The traditional division of roles with the manager as the negotiation leader and the different experts in charge of each their part functions poorly. The customer asks the supplier: 'Is it possible to equip the data system with more functions which make day-and-night work possible?' Before the negotiation leader on seller's side has had time to formulate the necessary questions about the customer's new needs, the systems specialist takes over: 'We have already done that for another customer and his system works very well. We do not need to make new changes in order to equip your system with similar functions'. The sales manager saw an opportunity to sell and once again receive payment for the expertise built up, but in his eager to demonstrate how clever he is, the systems specialist has given it all away for free.

In order not to fall into the trap, they should have done as follows.

Until the group has been properly welded together and a natural and well-functioning role division has set in, the negotiators should maintain a strict discipline and divide the roles in a different way, as explained below.

- **A negotiation leader.** Choose the one who is best with words and not automatically the most senior person. In principle, the negotiation leader is the only one who talks. The negotiation leader does not have to be the boss.

- **A listener and an observer.** Choose a negotiator who has sufficient experience to follow and understand the negotiation game. This person can, if possible, sit somewhat away from the negotiation table and take continuous notes. During each break it is the observer's job to provide the others with a picture of how the negotiations are progressing, what signals the opponent is sending out, and how the opponent has reacted to the negotiation leader's own propositions. The negotiation leader must be able to use the observer for summaries during the negotiations.

- **Someone who manages 'the economy'.** What have we given away? What have we got in return? What does the opponent's demands entail? How large a scope is left? Where are we now in the negotiations in relation to our goals?
- **The possible experts.** Who do you need to address on different issues? The group must decide how they want to communicate internally during the negotiations. Should they pass messages? Can they whisper or do they need to take breaks?

The group must agree that before anyone other than the negotiation leader speaks, he must be given a signal from the leads.

If the leader strays onto thin ice, becomes too aggressive, or finds himself in a situation where he has no answer, the others should intervene to suggest a break.

The group must agree to have a break prior to all important decisions where everybody can speak.

They are afraid of bargaining

Bargaining is the Achilles' heel of many negotiators. They avoid conflicts and during the bargaining phase they are forced to take up mutually contradictory perceptions of what a reasonable offer should look like. For this reason many negotiators are afraid of entering into this conflict and making offers, counter offers and bargaining. Their negotiations get stuck. Instead of making offers and counter offers they bury themselves in generally formulated arguments where they do not need to express themselves in a precise manner. Already known arguments are presented once again with no result.

All negotiations have a deadline, and when negotiators realize that they lack time, they force their offers and counter offers through. A ketchup effect arises where the entering of the agreement is often characterized by negotiators not knowing whether the agreement which they have entered into lies within the scope of their authority.

In order not to fall into the trap, they should have done as follows.

A better preparation where they have considered what an appropriate opening offer may look like, and how to bargain about the individual questions, e.g. 'Presupposing a significant price reduction, we can offer an advance payment'. They must also have considered what they mean by a significant price reduction. What should they add to their opening offer – goal – pain threshold? We want nine per cent interest on our investment so that is why we start demanding 11.5 per cent and would accept 7.5 per cent if absolutely necessary. This is where the so-called timetable can help (see Appendix 1).

The fear of making an offer has to be eliminated. The attitude that bargaining is something nasty must be revised. The available negotiation time must be organized in such a way that bargaining can get started at an early stage. The negotiators have to get used to taking breaks so that they can evaluate, at their own leisure, the opponent's offer and formulate their own.

They do not set up a strategy

Instead of approaching an agreement methodically and step by step, there are many who improvise. It is not clear to them when it is time to stop arguing and start moving on to map out the negotiation possibilities. They have no idea how and when it is time to make new offers or counter offers. They are not sure whether they should make one overall offer which covers all parts of the agreement, or whether they should take care of the problems one at a time.

They fail to see the clear line in the negotiations between showing openness and searching for the added value and assuming a tougher attitude when the added value is to be distributed.

They have not had a discussion about the advantages and disadvantages of being the first to make an overall offer instead of waiting for the opponent to do so. This means that the negotiations become unstructured and more characterized by verbal fights than creative problem solving. The negotiators reach impasse. Stress and insecurity grow. Instead of taking a break, many are faced with the choice between fighting or running away. The negotiators who run away commit the fatal mistake of making one-sided concessions. Those who stand up and fight make the negotiations into a zero-sum game. They do not listen to the alternatives being presented, and therefore the added value will not be utilized.

In order not to fall into the trap, they should have done as follows.

They should have carried out better preparation, where the negotiators have a clear idea of how they, step by step, can come closer to an agreement. The strategy can take many different forms. See Appendix 2 for more ideas.

They lose their grip on the economics

After 60 minutes of negotiation, poor negotiators may no longer know where they stand in relation to their own pain threshold or their chosen negotiation goal. They could just as well be over as under the pain threshold. They enter into too many part agreements and lose the grip on the overall economics of the deal. They enter into an agreement without knowing whether they have achieved a good result or whether they have landed outside their budget. In other words, their decision has been hasty.

There are several reasons for this: speed-blindness, insecurity or lack of a clear strategy. There is no one in the group whose job it has been to make calculations with respect to the deal and figure out how changes affect the overall economy. It happens even when the negotiation team consists of three or four people, and there is one in the group whose job it is to control the economy. I often meet well-educated people such as graduate engineers and bachelors of commerce with many years of business experience who can no longer calculate $7,850,000 + 3 \times 150,000 - 50,000 + 200,000$. The stress which they experience in connection with the negotiation becomes so overwhelming that they cannot make use of their knowledge.

Many people have forgotten the art of mental arithmetic, and they feel disabled when they have no access to a pocket calculator. They have a poor overview of the negotiations and the different pieces of the puzzle. They are stressed because they lack time. They are not used to handling overall solutions and comparing alternatives with different contents. Instead the suppliers are forced to adapt their offer so that the solutions become identical and thus easy to compare. The buyer justifies this by saying 'You cannot compare apples with pears'.

In order not to fall into the trap, they should have done as follows.

They should have chosen one person in the group to be in charge of the calculations. They should have taken a break to figure out, at their own leisure, what the consequences of the changes would be, without the stressing presence of the opponent. They should have made use of the timetable to get an overview.

They make insultingly low offers

The explanation of many insultingly low offers is miserliness and a poor analysis of what the opponent will think is a reasonable offer. Some negotiators overestimate their position of power, and they have a blind faith in starting out tough and then later finding a compromise where they back down from their unrealistic level. The other party must think that he has 'won' the game of 'give-and-take' or that it is fair or acceptable for both parties to meet half way.

This may be a success if the negotiators are inexperienced or the opponent is weak and has no alternative. Most people who have been presented with an insultingly low offer feel offended and break off all further negotiation. Others remain seated but with their guards up. This derails the negotiation and the parties end up with a trade-off where the added value is not utilized at all.

In order not to fall into the trap, they should have done as follows.

You have to realize that insultingly low offers have no place in constructive negotiations with the aim of establishing a partnership. You have to try to put yourself in the opponent's place and ask the question 'How would I react if I got this offer?'

They do not accept that the opponent makes money

Poor negotiators might turn down advantageous propositions because they believe the propositions to be unfair. For example, a company which ran into legal problems in connection with a project approached a mediator for help. Their lawyer told them that they most likely would lose if the opponent chose to go to court to solve the conflict. The loss may amount to $500,000.

The mediator is willing to assume the job provided that the client accepts all settlements up to $500,000.

In response to the client's question about what he charges per hour, the mediator says 'I do not charge by the hour. The risk of me failing is probably significant, and in that case I charge nothing. But if I succeed in landing a deal within the agreed economic frame and the settlement costs you, say, $300,000, there is $200,000 up to your pain threshold. Of that amount I charge half, i.e. $100,000.' The client finds this unreasonable and says 'But imagine that you work less than ten hours on the case. Do you then seriously believe that you should be paid $10,000 an hour?'. Instead of looking at the alternative, viz. the likely cost of $500,000, you object violently and abstain from only paying $400,000.

You want to pay by the hour. If the hourly rate is reasonable, you have no trouble accepting that so and so many hours pass. The overall cost and the guarantee of a result are less important.

In order not to fall into the trap, they should have done as follows.

In this example, the negotiators should have learned to look at their second-best alternative when making a decision. If they do not accept the proposition on the table, what alternatives do they then have? What would they lose if they did not accept a solution which was profitable for the opponent? They should have swallowed their annoyance of letting the opponent make money on the deal.

They are not good at listening

Those who cannot or will not listen find no new openings, and therefore may fail to obtain not only new information but also a possible existing added value. Insecurity makes many stick stubbornly to their original plan no matter what happens at the negotiation table. Many are afraid of listening because it seems risky to them. Maybe they should re-evaluate their assessments and ideas of what makes a good proposition.

In order not to fall into the trap, they should have done as follows.

Choose one member of the group whose job it will be to listen. He must possess the art of listening, which is significantly more difficult than arguing. In the concept of listening is far more than simply receiving the opponent's words passively. These negotiators have to realize that they do not know the answer and that new information may get them to see entirely new possibilities.

Summary: Why negotiations fail

For many of the negotiators who fail it is a question of learning to think differently when they are preparing and analyzing their negotiations. They must dare to be active during the negotiations and use significantly more energy on mapping out the negotiation possibilities, and they must bargain instead of arguing. They need to improve their communication skills.

> For many of the negotiators who fail it is a question of learning to think differently when they are preparing and analyzing their negotiations.

But they will not automatically become better at negotiating simply by reading books and gaining a theoretical knowledge of negotiation. That is only the beginning. The negotiation skill can only be developed by means of practical negotiation exercises and by real negotiations.

We furthermore have to accept that not all people can learn the art of negotiating, and therefore others have to negotiate on their behalf. It is often a surprise to learn that there is a gulf between having a theoretical knowledge and insight into negotiation and being able to negotiate in a constructive manner. At the beginning of our courses most participants nod in agreement with much of what we say. They do not know the mistakes and the pitfalls. The advice we give them seems self-evident.

After a couple of hours they have to carry out their first negotiation exercise and this is when they realize that it is not as straightforward as they thought. It turns out that many of them are not used to analyzing the negotiations in a constructive manner. They are self-centred and do not give the opponent a thought; nor do they consider how he may view the negotiation. After about an hour's preparation, the group has come to an agreement about how to negotiate. They are often quite sure that they have found a good strategy.

However, as soon as they sit down at the negotiation table, they are confronted with a reality which they were not ready for:

- formal communication techniques,
- technical competencies;
- evaluation norms for the technical standard;
- choice of strategy;
- time factors.

All knowledge of what we have told them and insight into what they ought to do to achieve constructive negotiations have evaporated. The simple and self-evident appears difficult and remote.

The company CEO has a big responsibility. The organization and bookkeeping must be designed in such a way that the overall economy becomes visible. It must not be possible to manipulate the system and transfer costs to other accounts and several accounting years. Negotiations must be revised.

The employees are often too poorly educated. In today's slim organizations, everybody suffers from a lack of time. People without a commercial education are assigned to commercial negotiations before they have had time to acquire sufficient experience. Negotiation skills among employees are no better today than they were 20 years ago.

Other common mistakes

In connection with the real negotiations in which we have participated, we have also observed that the following are also common mistakes:

- the personal contact is forgotten;
- negotiators do not understand their opponents;
- they insult the opponent;
- other interested parties are overlooked;
- cost savings within one link of the chain are eaten up by problems within another;

- parties are excessively suspicious of each other;
- stinginess;
- keeping hold of territory;
- political value norms;
- envy;
- cultural differences;
- the 'us and them' feeling prevails.

Each of these is discussed in more detail below.

The personal contact is forgotten

The personal contact is forgotten when enquiries and offers are exchanged, which leads to misunderstandings. The opponent focuses his interest on the different points. Significant information is lost. Offers are automatically rejected because the price is too high. If the supplier's ideas of how to solve a problem do not correspond with the buyer's intentions, the offer is rejected.

It is not possible to express yourself so clearly in writing that misunderstandings can be avoided. For example, we let a group of hundreds of negotiators interpret the same enquiry, the same offer and the same agreement. The variations in the interpretation of an identical text are so great that participants have questioned whether the others who had interpreted the text in another way really had had the same text to look at.

In the technical requirement specification it reads: 'The machine capacity must be 100 units per minute'.

This might seem fairly unambiguous but that is not the case.

- When the opponent says: 'Must be', should that be interpreted as a non-negotiable demand or as a wish?
- Does *capacity* mean normal capacity or maximum capacity?
- How has the customer arrived at 100 units per minute? Do we know anything about the daily capacity, possible problems or the customer's future needs?

Only personal contact with the opponent can give us the answers and an understanding of the opponent's reasoning.

Far too many suppliers who have missed out on a deal have received the explanation that: 'We thought the others made a better proposal'. As supplier, you wonder why you were never given the chance of making an offer on equal terms. The customer has decided to carry out his project in another way than the one specified in the enquiry but you will never have the chance of showing what you can do.

Negotiators do not understand their opponent

Cultural clashes can take place even though the negotiators do not come from different nations. The entrepreneur meets the cautious economist. Men meet women. The bureaucrat meets the self-employed businessman. The city-dweller meets the villager. In connection with several negotiations at the highest level concerning projects worth billions and where a crisis situation suddenly has arisen, we have been called in as experts to try to get the negotiations back on track. Our clients have described their opponents in one of the following ways.

- 'They are civil servants who do not understand what they are dealing with. Anyone with just a little presence of mind can see that this is a project with great potential. They just try to consolidate their own positions. I do not understand why they have entered the project.'
- 'I am going crazy every time they start discussing details. I do not understand what they want. Are they in or on the way out of the project? They do not answer my questions.'
- 'I am going crazy. They fight and argue about every single detail. It is a matter of prestige all the time.'
- 'I just cannot stand the sight of their female lawyer. How she has ended up in their management group is completely beyond me. She is no good, interferes in everything and the others let her go ahead. I wonder if they are afraid of her.'
- 'I have offered to buy them out but they will not sell. They will not contribute the extra capital needed. They demand to remain on the management board but they will not do anything to help.'
- 'We do not understand their chief negotiator. We do not know what it is he wants. His predecessor was a person you could talk to.

He was really interested in making it a good project. This one just sits looking at us without saying anything. We have never met such a strange person.'

Things reach a deadlock if the human chemistry is not compatible. We can often talk our way towards a compromise on technical solutions, distribution of risks and economic conditions. If, however, it does not work out between the people, the negotiations will fail even though the technical and economical prerequisites are in order. If another group of people had met around the same negotiation table, the problems would never have arisen. We must be culturally compatible.

It is difficult to distinguish between the case and the person. The controller who questions the cost budget and the visions in a project instead of unquestioningly accepting the estimated profits is just doing his job, but we perceive his critical questions as an attack on our competence and our grand ideas. A more cautious choice of words than direct brutal criticism may be the solution: 'I can see that there is significant potential here which makes the project interesting but how can we be sure that…'.

Often both parties lack communicative competence, which is why justified questions and criticism are perceived as personal attacks. He who feels criticized is not able to take a step back and realize that the criticism is about things in the project and not about him as a person. Our emotional reaction becomes strong and we cannot control it. The animosity and the feeling of alienation between us increase. In such a situation it is much easier for the outside expert to remain emotionally neutral, to look at the matters of the case and try to make the parties respect each other.

They insult the opponent

When the negotiators prepare themselves for important negotiations, they often exaggerate their own effort, costs, risk and importance. At the same time they try, by means of arguments, to make the opponent's effort, costs, risk and importance seem less. Behind this may be a need to appear strong in front of their own employees or sympathizers. It is especially common among politicians. They have many goals which they want to fulfil within the frames of one and the same negotiation.

Those whose arguments are based on a position of strength cannot see how their arguments insult the opponent. They enter the negotiations with a strong conviction of being unique whereas the opponent can easily be replaced. The negotiators position and express themselves in the following ways.

- 'We do not see why you as a lecturer have to have insight into our calculations. It is our idea and you are just our sub-contractor.'
- 'Why should we listen to you? We decide how to market this, and whether we want to supply any details of your participation or mention your name in our brochure is entirely up to us.'
- 'Any of your competitors can do this, too, so why should we choose you? We can actually buy this competence at Manpower!'
- 'Your only contribution is an old customer file; we are the brains behind the project.'
- 'This will not cost you anything; it is just old leftovers you contribute.'
- 'It is very risky for us to work with you. What if you don't perform satisfactorily?'
- 'We have to look at this in a businesslike manner, and we cannot allow you to have direct contact with the end customer. It is our customer and you are just our sub-contractor.'

These are insults which can stir up feelings that are so strong that continuing the dialogue becomes impossible. Often the insult is not deliberate. The negotiators do not spend time wondering how their choice of words and argumentation are perceived by the opponent. They do not care.

The insult is the consequence of ill-considered and aggressive use of words. When the opponent presents an idea, you answer: 'You are wrong; this would not work. Technical problems would arise which you should have thought of'. Instead of focusing the discussion on the contents of the proposition, the initiator is criticized for being wrong. An alternative choice of words would be: 'It is an interesting and exciting idea but if I understand you correctly we also have to consider where to place the main unit to avoid heat generation problems. Do you have any suggestions as to how we can overcome that problem?'

All merger attempts between Telia and Telenor fell through in 2000, mainly because the politicians involved were unco-operative and aired their political beliefs — a well-known method of creating conflicts and insults. We shall not easily forget how the Swedish minister of trade, Björn Rosengren, expressed his own value norms and his frustration over the opponent being difficult to negotiate with. He named them the 'last Soviet state', on public television and succeeded in insulting the entire Norwegian nation.

When we are tired, frustrated and stressed, it is best that we keep silent or else we will reveal the true picture of what we feel and think of the opponent. Freudian slips do not benefit co-operation. The experienced negotiator withholds his own value norms; he has learned from the defence and finds 'the situation satisfactory'.

Other interested parties are overlooked

The parties at the negotiation table can agree completely that the deal is excellent, but have they remembered to take the other interested parties into consideration? Many transactions have to be kept secret until all the pieces are in place. What would the employees most likely to be affected by the deal think? Is the agreement like a cold shower or a threat? If yes, how can we achieve an understanding and active participation in order to meet the business objectives?

The other interested parties include employees, customers, suppliers, banks, owners, authorities and other partners. The mass media and the academics seem to be able to influence things. These groups can have an influence which surprises many people. The Volvo/Renault deal fell through because the shareholders' national union mobilized resistance to it.

Cost savings within one link of the chain are eaten up by problems within another

In the 1970s, with the aim of reducing production costs per vehicle, one Swedish car manufacturer decided to leave the quality control of the finished car to the customer. At the same time the last production stage was moved out of the factory and over to the dealers' garages. Defects which the customers discovered on their new cars should be handled by the garages and fixed within the warranty year.

Only when the car had covered 10,000 km and the customer had discovered all defects and after the garage had corrected them, was the car considered finished and entirely delivered.

The car manufacturer did not inform the customers about the new concept and had no accept from them. All the gains should go to the producer. It was a disaster. The customers were outraged. The garages spotted a chance to make money from the producer and started to repair invented as well as real defects. People started to question whether the trade mark was a sign of quality.

Another Scandinavian example is the development of the public health service, particularly in Sweden and Denmark. Economies of scale are praised and defended tooth and nail by certain politicians and bureaucrats. The Swedish and Danish public health service no longer functions in a humanitarian way. Nor is it cost or resource efficient. Those responsible for it lack the ability to see things from a holistic perspective. The public health service has grown into an incredibly big, black hole which swallows more and more money while producing fewer and fewer health services.

The high price which we have to pay for the public health service is not caused purely by taxation. Added to the price must be the number of patients who die due to lack of treatment, needless suffering as a consequence of long waiting lists, burned out staff, worn down relatives who are forced to nurse their ill family members when the public health service no longer functions. Efficiency is measured in terms of the number of patients per doctor or the number of treatment days per diagnosis, and it says very little about how the treatment really works and what it costs. No holistic perspective is applied to explain how the money a county councillor/economist can save by shutting down wards and hospitals returns as multiplied costs in the shape of greater sufferings, greater absence due to illness, waiting hours, costs for the relatives who cannot do their job, and premature death because all this has not been included in the calculation.

Sadly, those who have authority over this public business have not been able to perceive their propositions from a socio-economic point of view.

Parties are excessively suspicious
of each other

Being naive in connection with business transactions and different kinds of co-operation can be costly. We have to follow our intuition if we get a feeling that the proposition we are presented with sounds too good to be true. Sleep on it, and consider whether all the facts are on the table. It may be a sign of warning if the opponent in different ways tries to force an agreement. It is something else to exhibit exaggerated suspiciousness and assume that everybody is out to cheat and deceive you. The scepticism you then signal can make many otherwise honest partners refrain from doing business with you.

Stinginess

The stingy negotiator violates the opponent's legitimate need to get his fair share of the cake. Stinginess often results in an argument that the opponent finds insulting. He has a feeling of not being treated as an equal partner. It is even worse if the stinginess is backed up by a case showing that the distribution you favour is fair.

A partnership which works has taken both parties' interests into consideration. As negotiators we face a dilemma. We must have the courage to be open and provide the opponent with a good picture of our situation and our prerequisites. This is necessary in order to find and realize the likely added value. There has to be an incentive for the opponent to dare react with a similar openness and find the partner-ship meaningful. The incentive is part of the added value which we create. At the same time it is our job to challenge the limits of the opponent and not give away more than necessary. The stingy person cannot manage the balancing act between being naive and being stingy, i.e. being businesslike.

We often recommend that negotiators put themselves in the opponent's place: 'How would they experience and react to their own offer and argumentation?'

The time which some people spend on trying to reach better and better agreements bears no reasonable proportion to the gains they acquire. Finally the opponent gets tired. Instead of landing a good deal, they are forced to start all over again and look for new partners.

Keeping hold of territory

A patient with a leg sore gets a visit from the district nurse to have it treated. She discovers that the sore has become infected. She has known the patient for a long time and knows that antibiotics are needed. Does the health service then let the most cost efficient and best qualified person handle the job and write out the prescription? Is the nurse allowed to give the patient the medicine he needs? Usually not. She has to contact the doctor in charge and tell him what she has seen and what diagnosis she has arrived at. The doctor who has not even seen the patient writes out a prescription which is subsequently dispensed at the pharmacy to some one from the home care system who visits the patient the next day.

The district nurse would have been able to handle this in a cost-efficient way without endangering the patient's health. But things are not done that way.

Where is the problem? Many doctors claim that the nurses lack the necessary knowledge to write out prescriptions. If that is true, they should receive further training. The real problem is the large group of people who zealously guard their territory. They fight any redistribution of work and responsibility with every available means. A great deal of the Scandinavian health service problems, for example are organizational and not due to lack of money.

Political value norms

Statistics show that treatment at a private clinic often is cheaper than the public health service. Political value norms and the guarding of preserves put a spoke in the way of making the public health service more efficient. So far only treatment scandals, long waiting lists and election years have resulted in other parties with different value norms taking over and making the people in charge redistribute the means and buy services from those with the lowest production costs. We have to learn to look at the totality, that the patient is getting better and that the costs to society are being reduced. You cannot be appalled by the fact that the private practitioner can make money at the same time by exercising a profession which is more effective than the public service. You should also listen to how the employees see their work situation in the public and the private health sector respectively.

In the private industry there is a term for letting the best suited person handle a job — outsourcing. We must concentrate our resources on the things we are best at and let others handle the additional services. We need to run our company in an effective way.

Envy

The average health service waiting lists are long. What happens in some countries during coffee breaks? All employees, even doctors and psychologists, who are hired to take care of the treatment of the ill, have days where they are responsible for coffee making, buying cakes for coffee, cleaning the coffee room and watering the plants. They are not off the hook. That it is the patients who suffer does not worry the envious people. In the former Soviet Union everybody who wanted accommodation had to do 500 hours' building work. A professor or doctor can always carry bricks.

Cultural differences

In negotiations where the parties represent different cultures, the risk of insults, misunderstandings and mutual distrust grows. The negotiators have to learn to be aware of and able to handle the cultural differences which manifest themselves. In the negotiations between Telia and Telenor we were given countless examples of how the cultural differences between Norway and Sweden and between businessmen and politicians finally made the merger impossible. If experienced politicians and businessmen keep intervening, creating value norm conflicts and making the parties' blood boil, what will then happen when the employees are to mark their new territories?

Our experience from thousands of negotiations shows that if the personal chemistry is lacking between the involved negotiators and future partners, then it is virtually impossible to reach a co-operation agreement which will work in the long term. The parties' energy will instead be focused on a fight where success only can be gained at the expense of the opponent.

We have probably all participated in meetings where everything fell into place immediately or meetings where we were on guard from the very beginning or rejected the opponent. What is personal chemistry? The first time we meet someone new, we interpret the signals we pick up with our eyes, nose and ears in a matter of seconds. Based on our previous experience, knowledge and preconceived opinions, our perception of the opponent is cemented. Our reaction tells more about us than about the opponent but influences the result of our negotiation. Dare I trust my feelings or should I give other people a chance instead of allowing my own preconceived opinions or random circumstances to control my decisions?

What is communication?

Two CEOs from BUILD Constructions Ltd. in Copenhagen are visiting Intropia PLC, a large listed pharmaceutical firm in London. They want to sell a new industrial and commercial building located in London's expanding business centre, Canary Wharf. Before the meeting a lot of correspondence has taken place. The BUILD Constructions Ltd. CEOs have written that they have a number of the country's leading companies as clients and would like very much to see Intropia PLC as a future partner.

Intropia calls the meeting and recommends that BUILD Constructions Ltd. bring a professional negotiator and a lawyer. The two CEOs arrive at the meeting in the traditional Scandinavian relaxed attire, i.e. white socks, Ecco shoes, colourful shirts and windcheaters and matching short ties. The Intropia PLC representatives are wearing dark suits, shiny leather shoes and discrete ties.

When they meet in the conference room the Intropia representatives politely, but routinely, ask: 'How are you?' without really expecting an answer. They are told that one of the BUILD Constructions Ltd. CEOs has some stomach problems and that the other suffers from too much work.

The sales manager from BUILD Constructions Ltd. takes a bottle of Schnapps out of his briefcase to start the meeting in a relaxed manner. The Intropia representatives politely, but firmly, state that the company is an alcohol-free area and declined. 'We did not know; you must be bored... haha!', the BUILD Constructions Ltd. people respond whereupon one of them produces a packet of cigarettes. ' I am sorry but we are also a non-smoking organization', the Intropia leader says.

The BUILD Constructions Ltd. people quickly look at each other but continue steadily to take their proposition out of the briefcase. 'The construction work can be ready by December 2003', the project leader starts out, 'and we wanted to hear whether you want in?'

'Do you have drawings and surveys which you can present on transparencies or on the board?' asks Intropia.

The BUILD Constructions Ltd. people quickly look at each other again: 'Well ... no, is that necessary now..?'

Now it is the Intropia representatives' turn to look at each other!

One of the BUILD Constructions Ltd. CEOs reacts quickly. It is obvious that he is the most communication minded, when he pulls a presentation brochure out of a bag from the local discount shop. 'Here is some information about the purpose and the idea but there are no drawings!'

'Can you draw the layout on the flip chart?', asks Intropia. 'Well .. no...yes .. but I can try', answers the technical manager from BUILD Constructions Ltd.

This fictional example illustrates the countless choices which life gives us in the thousands of communicative situations which we, deliberately or not, find ourselves in every single day.

Communicative competence will make you stronger within the following common areas:

- personal motivation;
- personal communication;
- meeting techniques;
- presentation techniques.

These are things which every professional businessperson needs in everyday life, some more than others, of course.

Do you know the situation where you face a type of person who makes you feel belittled? We call it personal chemistry and it can be either physical or psychological. During the meeting this person insults your thoughts, attitudes, ideas and objectives. You may be accommodating and leave the meeting annoyed, feeling: 'My idea was the best!' but for some reason you were not able to assert yourself. How do you manage to stand by your rights, ideas and objectives without others insult you or your interests? By means of assertive behaviour.

How did you react the last time your boss or colleague asked you to present the new proposition to the customer?

Did you think 'Oh, no why me, what shall I do?' Did you ask your boss 'Is it not better that someone else does it?' Were you insecure, unprepared, and without the faintest idea of the objective and how to handle the presentation?

Were you terribly nervous before the presentation? Were you unable to sleep at night, and did you make your presentation shaking all over?

Consider a number of other situations. Have you experienced a lecture where the lecturer was a brilliant cure for insomnia? He spoke with a monotonous voice, made no movements but clung to the lectern while looking down on his pile of papers and you thought: 'Please be over soon!'

During the break you meet a business connection who gives you a limp handshake, looks down at the floor while he loudly says: 'Nice to meet you.'

You were negotiating with your supplier last month. You agreed on how to send the delivery, its contents and the composition of the price.

Your supplier has now delivered the product to the wrong place with the wrong contents and at a too high price. What went wrong with your agreement? After all, you did agree?

At the internal meeting every Friday you are used to the fact that Richards constantly interrupts everybody else. Olsson minds his own business and is never engaged in the discussions. Ms. Morris on the other hand is very engaged but only when it comes to talking to her neighbour Mrs. Rachel, who thinks Bob, the boss, is incompetent and that his ideas are useless.

You are also used to seeing that eight of out ten meetings amount to nothing. At best they lead to a conclusion that will never be realized. What is missing?

The above-mentioned facts are common features for a number of businesspeople, from project managers, CEOs, sellers, buyers to technicians.

The four areas do not comprise a theory which we can learn in school, in business college, at the university or the business school. They are most often learned in real life under the motto 'Trial and Error', hopefully with as few errors as possible, otherwise you would risk being fired.

- Personal motivation
- Personal communication
- Meeting technique
- Presentation technique

This insight will improve and motivate your own self-esteem and self-confidence and result in better communicative skills within a number of different areas. Good ideas and genius have too often been lost in unattractive packaging.

Personal motivation is perceived very differently. To some people it has an even negative ring to it: Manipulation or misuse. Others are attracted to it. What sort of personal motivation do you want? Persuasive abilities? What does personal motivation mean to you?

Throughout history, personal motivation has been how we control our lives, carry out our ideas and convince others. This is achieved first by means of our physiology; he who was the strongest physically and the quickest had the power to control the others. Gradually as civilization developed, the personal thrust came from inheritance. The king and his armies ruled others through their symbols of power.

At the beginning of the industrial age, capital was the decisive factor of power. Without solid capital, you had neither opportunities, nor influence nor power. Capital was power. Those with access to it dominated.

The above-mentioned things still play a role in our lives today. It is better to have money than to be poor. It is better to be physically strong than small and weak. But the biggest personal resource today is knowledge.

We live in a time where new thoughts, ideas and opportunities change the world almost on a daily basis. We receive with the speed of light a huge, almost incomprehensible, amount of information consisting of books, TV, radio, Internet, newspapers, magazines, etc. In this world the people with the information and the ability to communicate it will have the things kings used to have: unlimited power and personal motivation.

The truth is, however, that even in this day and age information is not enough. If we only needed good ideas and creativity, we would live differently. Performance or action is what produces results. Knowledge is only a potential force until it finds its way to a person who understands to use it efficiently and correctly.

What are the things we form an opinion of in no time?

- facial expressions;
- posture;
- eye contact and handshake;
- how the opponent greets us;
- appearance;
- clothing;
- voice and language;
- smell/hygiene;
- gender;
- age;
- skin colour.

We can affect and do something about most of this ourselves provided that we are motivated and mature enough to want meetings with new people to go smoother. We should not wipe out our own personality but we should not expose ourselves to the risk of being judged without first being heard either. If we are accepted, we will also get the chance to be seen and heard. If the opponent has judged us in advance because of his value norms and preconceived opinions, we will never get the chance. In that case our meetings become a protest — but a protest without greater meaning.

The lack of social competence can create many unnecessary negotiation problems. In the situations where we cannot or will not do something about the signals we send out, we can send a colleague instead in order not to create unnecessary problems.

Be aware of the cultural differences existing within your own country, including:

- women/men;
- city/village;
- technicians/economists/humanists;
- young/old;
- company cultures;
- private/public company;
- politicians/their voters.

Checklist: International negotiations

Below follows a list of the areas you must pay attention to and check for cultural differences. The checklist is taken from our negotiation hand book *The Negotiation Manual*, used in our seminars and which goes through the respective points.

1 Negotiations fail if the inter-human relations between the parties do not work.
   - How do you dress?
   - Territory and bodily contact.
   - Relationships between men and women.
   - Men/women — two different cultures.
   - Meals.
   - Gifts.
   - Perception of time.
   - Learn to talk about the weather.
   - Negotiating in a foreign language.
   - Individual contra the group.
   - Forms of address, names, titles and age.
   - Religion and politics.
   - Trust.

2 Important areas besides the inter-human relations between the parties.

- Legislation.
- Economic characteristics.
- Infrastructure.
- Bribery and other ethical questions.

In order to gain more knowledge of different cultures, of what is right and wrong in different countries, you could read *Understanding Global Cultures*, (ISBN 0761913297) by Martin J. Gannon.

3 The 'us and them' feeling

One of the most important tasks for a partnership management is to eliminate the 'us and them' feeling. The two people who enter into a partnership become one. If that is to become a reality, it requires an open mind and a great effort to build a new joint identity.

If tough negotiations have taken place prior to the co-operation, with bosses and owners fighting about power, structure and location, there is a risk that they have openly shown suspicion for each other. This may have rooted itself in the respective companies. Those who feel like losers of course want to get even. According to CEO Fred Hassan that was the biggest problem when Swedish Pharmacia merged with US-based Upjohn. The new group came to consist of three companies with significant mistrust between them: an American, an Italian and a Swedish company. That ended up affecting the share prices negatively, and it took the group two years to restore the share price.

3
Distrust costs millions

'Distrust costs millions' said the heading of an article in a leading European newspaper. The article was about the decisive factor in business life — the human one.

We can train, learn, study, practise and try to use all the tools which we learn in this book. But none of them will be conveyed or create efficient results without a basic and absolute trust in you as a businessman, negotiator and partner.

When we advise our clients, we may at times come across a negotiator who tells the truth, the whole truth and nothing but the truth but who becomes seriously distrusted by his opponent. Why?

Would you trust your financial adviser if he wore a floral shirt with a Mickey Mouse tie, or if someone you interviewed had a big tattoo visible?

> Would you trust your financial adviser if he wore a floral shirt with a Mickey Mouse tie, or if someone you interviewed had a big tattoo visible?

As mentioned in Chapter 2, there are a number of features which we notice within the first seven seconds of meeting a person we have never seen before. What is it that stimulates these feelings within this short space of time. If you had to set your impressions down on a list, it would very likely contain their facial movements, eyes, carriage, intonation and clothing.

Image can make the difference between the win or lose situation. Image is how others perceive you, not the way you perceive yourself.

A number of the topics which we touch upon in this chapter applies to both your own behaviour and your interpretation, translation and understanding of other people.

Two-thirds of all jobs go to people who are skilled in the interview situation rather than to those who are skilled candidates.

The Carnegie Institute of Technology has published a study which very often provokes a number of our clients:

15 per cent of your success is based on your technical/specialist knowledge and around 85 per cent is based on knowledge of human behaviour...

Imagine that you play on a football team. The teams playing do not know the rules, the score system and do not know which team is ahead. During the interval the coach says to you that all you need to do is concentrate on playing ball. What would this do to your motivation and trust? Of course, that has disappeared with regard to the coach and with regard to the task.

The same applies to the business life. If people do not know whether they are winning or losing, we risk a total loss of motivation and enthusiasm.

Consider this situation. You participate in a very exhausting expedition in the Amazon rainforest. Each morning you are told how far to go and what to carry. When you ask the leader where you are going, he answers: 'I am afraid I cannot tell you; it is classified information and besides it is not relevant to you!'

There are four levels of trust relationships, which should be functional in companies and in people:

- relationships with customers;
- relationships with suppliers;
- vertical relationships between managers and employees;
- lateral relationships between departments and divisions.

Within our courses in negotiation technique, we operate with the 'win-win' concept. A foundation which presupposes trust between the parties in order to be able to create added value. Studies carried out on the basis of more than 22,000 negotiators in more than 1,000 negotiations show that in the traditional negotiation (distrust) more than 40 per cent of the potential added value is thrown away. Put another way, in a deal with a frame of $1 million, $400,000 is potentially lost due to lack of trust and communication.

> Try to imagine that you could trust all people. The workman who says that he will come on Friday actually comes on Friday. Your colleague who promises to finish the report on Monday in fact finishes the report on Monday. The person who says that you will get the cheque tomorrow actually mails it.

The biggest problem for all negotiators is to trust the opponent, i.e. opening up and passing on information.

That you prefer to do business with the people you like, trust and feel solidarity with than find someone who corresponds to your technical and economic needs may seem irrational but it only shows that your psychological needs are more important than your material needs and for this reason your decision is then from our point of view rational.

The person who aims at creating a positive negotiation climate and openness and who wants to gain his opponent's trust tries to:

- listen;
- answer questions;
- be open and show his body language;
- express interest;
- respect the opponent's opinions.

It is unfortunately normal for negotiators to work with unnecessarily expensive solutions. The resources go up in smoke and none of the parties see any benefit. Furthermore, a relationship that is lacking leads to a poor negotiation climate where the parties express lack of trust and openness towards each other.

When it comes to making decisions on the terms that they are to ask for or accept, lack of openness leads to negotiators only considering what they can gain from the terms. They are lacking and have not tried to obtain information about what the terms will entail for the opponent. The decision leads to sub-optimizing. They do not make use of the possibilities for rationalization and optimal distribution of existing costs and gains.

Do not perceive demands as threats. Behind them there may be possibilities of added value if they are used correctly. In order to find out whether this is the case, you should use another technique rather than opposition. You need to get a constructive dialogue going.

Deceit is widespread

A study by the University of Virginia in the US shows that lies are part of one in every five ten-minute conversations. Educated, middle class people lie even more frequently; on average in every third conversation.

It is believed that the difference is due to a better education, a better vocabulary and a sense of security that make it easier to lie. At the same time, people with a certain education level can see more easily the advantages which a well-placed lie can give and they are thus also more inclined to bend the truth somewhat.

Amongst other things, the study shows that 68 per cent of men would lie or cheat to get a job while 62 per cent of the women would do the same.

The American psychologist Paul Ekman has been studying lies for 25 years and he finds that it is easy to find out if people are lying most of the time. It has been documented through video recordings that our body gives us away over and over again. Only about 5 per cent of people have such a talent for lying that it cannot immediately be detected.

How can we tell if others are lying?

One of the most characteristic and the most easily recognisable features is touching of face or nose. It is an expression of 'assuring oneself'. We most often do it when we are lying or when we are very insecure by touching our cheek, lips, mouth or nose. One of the best known examples is probably that of former US president Nixon when he said in a TV speech 'I know nothing about the tapping of Watergate'. He touched his nose and covered his mouth.

Rubbing eyes buys us time and at the same time it no doubt also says that we are not particularly happy about what we are about to say. By rubbing eyebrows or forehead, we often try to increase the output.

Rubbing your ear may indicate stress in relation to the statement. Touching the neck usually also signals nerves just as frequent contact with your hair also expresses anxiety, confusion or stress.

Biting of nails, contact with watches, jewellery, buttons or nervously playing with coins or keys in your pocket are also indicators. Folding of arms over chest can express a need for self-affirmation. The use of pen as a pointing instrument or tapping indicates irritation or anxiety.

Eye contact is often lacking with the untrained or spontaneous liar. When lying or feeling insecure you have a tendency to look away. Other signals are frequent blinking which is a sign of nervousness, widening of your eyes or a profound stare, which is a conscious attempt to accommodate to the first point. By lifting your eyebrows you try to act surprised over the fact that you do not trust the person. The eye can in some cases be directed at the liar's top right corner as a sign of a constructed thought creation, i.e. not actual events but created scenarios.

A number of these signals (and others) may indicate lies or insecurity but they cannot alone be considered evidence. In order to create a congruent picture of lies or insecurity, more conditions must be co-ordinated in an overall conclusion.

Talking versus writing

Many people put something in writing when they should have appeared in person. And many people start talking where they ought to write a letter. But when should we do what?

Written communication goes directly to the brain's cerebral cortex, the highly developed analytical part of the brain. Oral communication contains feelings, expressions and energy and is therefore received by the creative part of the brain.

Written communication is a one-channel communication. We only satisfy visual perception. We take in the written communication word for word, line after line. Oral communication uses more channels, visual, audio and kinetic (feelings).

Written communication is well-suited for information of a specific factual character, i.e. data, details and other exchange of facts. Many people can read five times more quickly than they speak. You can concentrate your entire mind on the actual contents and you will not be distracted by a person's behaviour. You can read the material over and over again if you do not understand it or you can file it for later use.

If you want personal impact, influence and thrust and to be able to persuade other people, this must be done verbally with thrust. Written communication is almost the opposite of oral communication and it seldom has the capacity alone to convince people and thus change their attitudes and values.

Around 80 per cent of human communication is estimated to fall into the category 'persuasion', also called 'action-oriented communication'. This is used in connection with presentations, sales speeches, meetings and all situations where person A wants something done by person B.

When a seller wants to sell a new type of product, he does not send a letter. He comes in person thus getting his message across in a serious, sound and confidence-inspiring manner.

What prominent businessmen or politicians do you know who seem credible and appear serious and inspire confidence? When you meet a new person or watch a person make a statement on TV, they will most often be perceived as trustworthy or untrustworthy by you.

We cannot convey information and communication without inspiring people's confidence. People must trust what we say, as well as our contents and purpose. Our behaviour must put them at ease and make them understand the values we represent. This is done by means of congruent communication assisted by enthusiasm, self-confidence and energy.

Imagine that you are at a big marketing presentation. There are some 350 people present. The first speaker is introduced and starts. He walks on the stage, corrects his papers, many papers, and starts to read his speech. He looks down on the paper or at the floor. He speaks monotonously, without expression and has no body language.

You look surprised at him. He is renowned as a great expert in direct marketing. He does not sound like that. He does not seem particularly sure of his material and not at all like he is keen and enthusiastic on being there.

This speaker is, however, a renowned expert within his field. Just prior to the presentation he was talking with great charisma, self-confidence and enthusiasm to another colleague about new advances in their field. But on stage he is a sure cure for insomnia.

The next speaker is introduced. He uses big smart transparencies with colour and graphics. A powerful voice with variation, sympathetic insight and self-confidence. He walks around on the stage while he talks and gesticulates in time to his presentation. This was not what you had expected when you read the agenda. He is a market analyst and expert on market prognosis and statistics.

During the break you meet a new colleague, you shake his hand (he gives a limp handshake), talk briefly with him and he has limited eye contact. Your conclusion is clear; he will not last two months in the company. You do not register this consciously but his posture, body language and eye contact tell you a lot.

We constantly judge each other on our statements, opinions, appearance and behaviour which we will come back to.

> Companies with vision have realized that communication is a very important parameter when it comes to development of identity, profile and image.

Our total communication is the sum of the words we use, the tone of voice we use and the body language we express ourselves with. We call each of these levels *communication channels*.

If all three channels are identical in our communication it is called congruity, i.e. agreement between our expression and statement. At the same time communication trust is created.

I had dinner at the house of some friends once. When the wife came in. I said 'Hello Jane, how are you?' She stared at the floor and answered 'I'm fine'. I immediately registered that something was wrong. During dinner we talked about many things where she looked me straight in the eyes and was sure of herself but when we touched upon her personal life, she looked away.

The cause of the problem is irrelevant but this shows quite clearly how non-congruity, i.e. confusion between the communication channels, are picked up often unconsciously by the listener.

Studies have established that verbal communication, the words, represents 7 per cent of our total communication. Body language accounts for 55 per cent and word intonation for 38 per cent.

Non-congruity is, of course, the opposite if congruity. Jane, in the example above, displayed a non-congruent behaviour by sending out different messages through her body language, verbal language and intonation respectively. This channel confusion is picked up often unconsciously by you the listener.

Imagine that you are having a conversation with another person whom you are supposed to trust. He says: 'I would never lie to you!' While he says that, he is looking down at the ground. Would you believe him?

A scientific study based on a youth gang which robbed purses, watches and bags from people on public transport showed very clearly that one specific category of people was robbed.

The leader of the gang was interviewed for the study and one of the questions he was asked was how the gang defined its victim. 'We want the least possible trouble', he said 'so we go after the insecure one, the one who looks away, down on the ground or shows insecurity in his eyes or becomes scared when he sees us!'

This young man used his instinct to define his victim. He never chose the self-confident, upright person with a sure eye contact.

Conscious versus subconscious

Imagine a golf ball placed on top of a football. This illustrates the difference between subconsciousness in the shape of the football and the golf ball in relation to consciousness. The two consciousness levels are very different from one another but at the same time very dependent on each other.

The conscious mind can at a maximum contain 7 thoughts or actions at a time. Consciousness is used to identify information received through the six senses: vision, sound, taste, smell, touch or instinct.

The conscious mind registers and categorizes everything that goes on around you. Imagine that you are walking on a path in the forest, immersed in your own thoughts. Suddenly you hear a hissing sound and look down on the path in front of you in order to identify what has made the sound and see a snake.

The conscious mind now makes a comparison. The hissing sound you have just heard and the snake you have seen go to your sub-conscious mind where they are compared with previously stored information and experiences with snakes.

If the snake is four metres away and not very big, your subconscious mind tells you that there is no danger and that you can scare it off.

If the snake, on the other hand, has risen up, its fangs bared and ready to bite, you will receive a 'warning' message, which will stimulate your body's further action. The conscious mind has thus made an analysis before a decision is made. The conscious mind accepts or rejects data in connection with choices and decisions.

The subconscious

The subconscious mind is one big memory hard disk. The capacity is basically infinite. The subconscious mind stores everything that happens to you. When you are 21, you have already stored the equivalent of more than 100 times the contents of the entire *Encyclopaedia Britannica*.

The subconscious mind is one big memory hard disk. The capacity is basically infinite. The subconscious mind stores everything that happens to you. When you are 21, you have already stored the equivalent of more than 100 times the contents of the entire *Encyclopaedia Britannica*.

The purpose of the subconscious mind is to store and retrieve data. Your subconscious mind is subjective; it does not think and act on its own but acts on the basis of an order from your conscious mind. Your conscious mind decides and your subconscious mind obeys. Your subconscious mind has registered and stored that you body temperature is as it is and where your comfort zones are and how they function and work in order to keep you within your boundaries. Your subconscious mind makes you feel out of balance when you try something new or change the pattern of your behaviour.

Everybody likes to do what they know or think they are good at. This is called the comfort zone. This means that we live a very big part of our lives within this zone by doing things we know that we can do. We can also generally refer to this as self-confidence or self-awareness.

You can feel that your subconscious mind pulls you back to your comfort zone when you try something new, change job, call a new customer, meet a new person, etc.

The decisive difference between successful and less successful people is their ability to go further, to go beyond their comfort zone. They are aware of how quickly the comfort zone becomes a habit, and they know that enervating behaviour is an enemy to creativity and future possibilities.

In order to develop and change, you must be prepared to feel strange and different during the preliminary phase. If you are not prepared to feel clumsy or bad at the beginning of a new job, sport or in personal relations, you will be locked on a low success level.

Any idea or thought produced in your conscious mind will, without being questioned, be processed towards realization by the subconscious mind.

When you begin to believe that something is possible for you, your subconscious mind will begin sending out mental messages and energy. For example, if you decide to buy a red car, you will begin to see red cars everywhere and on every street corner. If you prepare a trip to a foreign country, you will begin to see articles and information about the country everywhere. Your subconscious mind draws your attention to the information, which may be necessary in your decision process.

When you begin to think of a new objective, your subconscious mind will take that as an order and begin to work towards fulfilling the objective. It begins by adjusting your words and actions in order to aim your behaviour at the target and become one with it. You are in fact working out a new comfort zone, or rephrased, a new habit.

When we create congruent behaviour, an agreement between what we say and the way we say it, we create credibility, trust and unique selling points (USPs).

By preparing ourselves as a USP, we have to look at different factors.

- **Our product:** That is ourselves. Is the quality in order? Are we self-confident? Do we believe in our own target and ability to live up to it?

- **Market position:** What are we aiming at? Who are our competitors, etc?

- **Packaging:** How do we present ourselves? How is our profiling perceived by other people? What signals do we want our marketing to send?

Stress

Physiologically, submissive and aggressive behaviour are conditions that cause stress. Submissive behaviour leads to remission in negotiation situations and aggressive behaviour leads to a combative attitude. Both types destroy productivity.

Imagine the tough Vikings. Our little Viking friend Thorleif is running in the big forest on the way home to his village.

He turns around a corner in a clearing. And there, suddenly is Gunhild, Thorleif's biggest enemy.

What are Thorleif's options now? He can run or fight. Submissive or aggressive behaviour respectively.

Assertive behaviour would be lethal for Thorleif. He could not start discussing Gunhild's basic rights and his respect for him in exchange for persuading him to let him go.

Stress is at the same time the foundation which affects us in modern society, in common business situations. In every negotiation stress is experienced more or less strongly and it affects us more or less.

Listen to your body's signals. When stress increases, the body will send out clear warning signals. Since all resources are mobilized for physical activity, your pulse will beat more quickly, you will breathe more heavily, you will begin to sweat and your muscles will tighten. Then it is high time to take a break.

The ability to act rationally is limited when stress situation affects you emotionally and when you feel insecure. In many conversations you will have an incomplete basis of information to make a decision. You try to meet threats, insecurity and stress by means of fight or escape. This is an incorporated behaviour which causes stress.

Your ability to evaluate is affected by your feelings. If you end up in a situation where you feel insecure or you are threatened or stressed, your rational thought process will short-circuit and you will respond with an emotional reaction, i.e. with fight or escape.

You are sitting waiting for some promised material from a colleague. He has forgotten his promise to you and when you remind him, he says: 'Sorry, I forgot. I can find it for you next week'. You get angry and answer: 'Do not bother. I can manage without your help'.

You make a rash decision instead of waiting despite the fact that you do have the time. If your decision later appears to be wrong and expensive, who will get the blame for that apart from your colleague?

Your ability to evaluate is affected by your feelings If you end up in a situation where you feel insecure or you are threatened or stressed, your rational thought process will short-circuit and you will respond with an emotional reaction, i.e. with fight or escape.

The only reasonable way of tackling stress is through breaks. Breaks during meetings buy us time. The break does not need to last three hours, it can be five minutes or less. The essential thing is to get away from the physical stress situation.

Physical symptoms

Different signals will tell you or your opponent whether a stress situation has occurred. It may be tensed or tight muscles, quicker breath, increase in blinking frequency, spontaneous and unstructured movements at the conference table, groaning, etc. Further signs may be increased swallowing, talking without air, licking of lips, clearing one's throat or smoking.

Besides the physical break, 3–10 minutes where you in fact leave the conference room, you can stall time while you are talking or during a meeting by:

- cleaning your glasses with a cloth while you think;
- removing your glasses;
- searching for a piece of paper in your bag;
- asking questions which are irrelevant to you but which require the opponent's concentration and answer but not yours.

When you are trying to read other people's body language during a negotiation, we can say that presumptions or decisions based on laziness most often is the sure way to failure. At the beginning you need to be very observant and perhaps only participate in the negotiation in order to observe the opponent's reaction pattern.

Remember that when you analyze another person's reaction, there is one thing missing, namely you. Other people adjust their reaction pattern to some degree conditional upon what types of people they meet.

We work specifically with the above-mentioned areas over several days in our training seminars and consultancy on communicative competence.

'You cannot learn to swim by simply reading a book.'

4
Why co-operation provides better solutions

An arrangement which is exclusively based on one party's victory over the other is barbaric and can never be humanized. It can only be maintained as long as the part who has the upper hand can force the opponent into submission. Sooner or later it will collapse. The alternative is co-operation and partnership. But the person who does not understand the theoretical reasoning behind the idea of partnership and added value, is not motivated to be open and run the risks inherent in a more open negotiation climate. In order to dare to co-operate, we must have accepted the theories.

The notion that two parties can increase their wealth by means of a rational division of labour is not in any way new. The idea was first advanced by Adam Smith at the end of the seventeenth century and further developed by David Ricardo at the beginning of the eighteenth century. The theories advanced by these two gentlemen showed that nations, companies and individuals may increase their wealth by creating added value.

To avoid new world wars in Europe, the Coal and Steel Union was founded in 1952 — a body strong enough to co-ordinate the activities within the coal and steel sectors and gain control over the armament industry. At the same time the intention was to make the production profitable and create new jobs. This became the basis for the EU we know today.

Two American scientists, W. Edwards Deming and Josef M. Juran, started to develop theories in the 1940s about how added value could be created through long-term relations with suppliers with the goal of obtaining a perfect production and deliveries on time. The ideas gained recognition in Japan where the car industry began to work with perfect components, just-in-time delivery, no stock, development of entire systems at the sub-contractors' and shorter productive time. The entire industrialized world conformed with different rationalization programmes. Not only the production but the entire business activity was dealt with, and we encountered new concepts such as business process re-engineering, outsourcing and strategic alliances.

The public sector follows. The company is subjected to competition, buy/sales systems are introduced, trade barriers disappear, a common currency is born in Europe, and the frontiers are opened up.

Since everybody is pursuing added value, everything becomes much tougher. We have to be a step ahead at all times. Ever greater skills are required of negotiators, technicians, project managers and business developers to keep competitors at arm's length. Two pairs of eyes and ears see and hear better than one pair. Two minds think better than one and can more easily see the synergies.

Two basic methods of creating added value

When two companies enter into a co-operation agreement, there will always be a certain amount of duplication of work. The extent of this can, however, be limited. It is, e.g. sufficient to have one finance department rather than two.

Whether the gain can be realized is determined by the extent to which the savings are being consumed because of territory conflicts and by the company's ability to dispose of the freed resources or make use of them in a productive way.

When the experience, the knowledge and the creativity which exist between the different people start to work together, a synergy effect arises. The sum of two plus two equals significantly more than four. These gains do not come about from nothing; they are dependent on the personal chemistry in the new constellation.

The physical work is transferred to the partner who can do it at the lowest cost. The realization of the gain depends on whether the company can dispose of the freed resources or make use of them in a productive way.

But what about all the small daily negotiations which are necessary for the company to function in accordance with the theories on value adding measures and in the plans which management has set up in the board rooms? How big a part of this added value is used? As discussed in Chapter 3, there are many who face problems and failure. The reality which we encounter at the negotiation table today shows how hard it is for these people to put the theories into real negotiation.

The uncertain and incomplete basis for decision making

When we try to find the solution to a problem, we rely on our experiences and the information which we have about the problem. The solutions which we come up with are then compared to our needs and a choice is made. We never have enough knowledge of the pieces of the puzzle at our disposal. Some information is incorrect. Our picture of reality is faulty and strongly influenced by preconceived opinions and value judgements.

Even if we had had every bit of information at our disposal, we would not have been able to calculate and compare all the thinkable alternatives. Just consider the fact that ten different pieces in a puzzle can be combined in 3,628,800 different ways. In order to be able to make a decision we take different shortcuts. We quickly decide on an alternative which we then fight for. Our will and ability to begin to listen to others then and embrace new information in order to test other solutions without prejudice may therefore be very weak. We evade the dialogue.

Co-operation is far from unproblematic. In fact, many constellations are impossible. There is no patent solution which automatically solves the problems and streamlines the activities. But when it works, we get better solutions for the following reasons.

• The co-operating parties act on a safer, more exhaustive and thus better basis for decision making. The quality of the decision is often proportional to the amount of information the parties have when they make their decisions.

• The increased amount means that they can see new alternatives. We often say: 'He found the missing piece of the puzzle,' if somebody sees the solution before the others.

- The increased amount of information means that the parties more easily discover which changes will lead to added value and which will make the project more expensive. The risk of making the wrong decisions is reduced.

- Parties who co-operate work more constructively. They do not waste energy on fighting about whose solution is the right one. They do not need to waste their time on flexing their muscles and running the risk of destroying the negotiation climate.

- They often act on a joint analysis of the situation. They spend their energy on finding the best solution together. The synergy effect which they then can obtain is well-documented.

- The parties may find that they have far more uniting needs than competitive needs.

- The parties complement each other and concentrate their resources in their individual areas.

Example: plasterboard

Many businesses keep doing things the old-fashioned way. They often enter into agreements lasting several years or framework agreements with incorporated suppliers whom they would like to continue to buy from. It is a practical way of simplifying purchases. In this example, we are dealing with the purchase of plasterboard for construction.

The yearly framework negotiation usually revolves around price, discounts and payment conditions. It is not necessary to negotiate about design and quality. The normal price for a large construction company is between $3.80–$4.15. The party which is the strongest at present tries to squeeze a few extra cents for himself. It is a traditional zero-sum game. If the construction company can squeeze the price down a few cents, the supplier has to cut into his own scanty gain.

If the buyer is going to succeed, he needs powerful reasoning: 'If you cannot accept a price level of about $3.40 for next year, we will be forced to buy the plasterboard in Poland. If we, the biggest construction company in this country, start to import Polish plasterboard, the other construction companies will soon follow. The Poles will then be able to sell such large quantities in Denmark that they can build up their own distribution facilities, and then you will have price competition everywhere. Do as we say and accommodate our demand for a price of $3.40, and you will not have to deal with the Poles'.

The supplier now has to choose between the devil and the deep blue sea. Many suppliers swallow their pride and sell at a too low price, which means that continuous production will not be profitable and not yield the return needed to develop the company. At best they will have bought themselves a little time.

In order to survive in the long run, the supplier may be forced to discontinue his production in Denmark and move it to Poland. We have countless examples of similar cases. Whether this moving-out of companies has been beneficial and created added value or whether it has been harmful depends on whose perspective it is seen from and how the restructuring has taken place.

Fortunately, the yearly negotiations on the price of plaster-board changed one year. Instead of focusing the entire negotiation on the price of $3.80–$4.15, the parties directed their attention to the total cost of fixing the plasterboard to the wall and making it ready for paperhanging. They acknowledged that the purchase price of plaster-board was insignificant when it is the total cost which determines whether the construction company can survive.

The total cost for fixing a plasterboard was $22.5, a cost which the construction company knew but never had questioned. The question which the parties asked themselves was: 'Can we bring the total costs down in one way or another?' Before the question could be answered, the parties had to get more information about what it was that made the costs go up. The progress of the plasterboard at the construction site was physically followed step by step from the time when the board was unloaded and until it was fixed to the wall. The following relevant facts were discovered.

- Many plasterboards are destroyed on the construction site. When the boards were unloaded, a truck or a wheelbarrow could rip the edge of a stack of boards before they were covered and many were destroyed during internal transport on the construction site. The total loss was in excess of 40 per cent. Because everybody knew that a plasterboard only cost $3.75, no one was really prepared to treat them carefully.

- The dimensions of the boards meant that it always took two men to carry a board.
- The dimensions of the boards meant that it was difficult and time-consuming to transport them on the construction site.

Today it seems that the same quantity of plasterboards, once finished and mounted, costs about $16.25. The parties have saved $6.25, which is significantly more than the cost of the individual board. This has been possible by:

- producing the boards in half the size; one man can now handle the board;
- by means of drawings, calculations of precisely how many boards are needed in every room are now carried out at the factory. Boards which need shortening can already be shortened to the right size at the factory. They are packed separately and lifted directly from the lorry through the window of the room in which they are going to be set up. The number of boards being destroyed during handling has been reduced significantly.

What is it that makes the creation of this great added value possible?

1. Instead of working towards your own goals, the biggest possible piece of the cake, you set up a new common goal: let us enlarge the cake before we share it. In this case: What can we do to reduce the total costs? As long as we only work towards our own goal — the biggest possible piece of the cake — a competitive situation is created where we spend our energy on finding the right arguments and then fighting about which arguments are the right ones. Instead of having a constructive negotiation, all forces are concentrated on the rhetoric. He who wins the verbal fight, gets a bigger piece of the cake. This victory is won at the expense of the opponent.

2. Because the parties focus on another goal, they also realize that they need significantly more information then they have themselves. Otherwise it will be difficult to find a new solution. When they choose to be open and to supply the opponent with their pieces of the puzzle, all parties get a better basis for decision making. They perceive the negotiation as a joint project where the goal is to find

the most cost-efficient solution, to minimize the risks and create improved earning possibilities. The quality of the solution is directly proportional to the amount of available and correct information.

3. After they had found the elements which pushed up the costs, the parties made use of their common experiences, abilities and creativity to find a new and better solution. The synergy gains which thus are made possible may be significant.

   Working methodically according to these three steps appears to be a matter of course and very simple, but our years of experience with negotiations indicate that there are not many negotiators who manage to accomplish this during real negotiations.

   Rationalizing a production process is not just about the old illustrious technical abilities. It is a prerequisite that there is chemistry between the people who have been chosen to solve the problem. Then we will have two parties who have an entirely different view of how to handle changes and negotiations. It is a basic prerequisite which is far too often missing in real life. Without this lubricant we will not get far with our technical abilities, creative thinking and ideas about business process re-engineering, and disputes will arise at the negotiation table.

   How is the gain going to be shared?

   The new method of manufacturing and delivering plasterboards gave the parties a new but more pleasant negotiation problem. Who is entitled to the rationalization gain of $6.25 which the parties have achieved together? A spontaneous, yet ill-considered suggestion is to share the gain equally. Why? The people suggesting a 50/50 split see this as a fair solution. Splitting the gain evenly is often a sign of fear of negotiating and bargaining, a fear which is characteristic of many negotiators. Many negotiators see a contrast between first having created an added value through co-operation and then afterwards being forced into a zero-sum game for the distribution of the added value.

   The parties have to learn to negotiate about the distribution in such a way that they do not give away too big a piece of the cake. It is all about keeping the biggest possible piece for yourself in order to be able to build up reserves and face an uncertain future. The opponent must be allowed to keep a sufficient amount to cover his part of the costs and the risks and to land a deal which is better than his alternatives. Whether a 50/50 distribution is too stingy or too generous, we will not always know. We expect that the opponent's demands and offers are negotiable but to which extent we do not know for sure.

Likely methods of sharing the cake include the following.

- Agree on the distribution in advance and how possible savings are to be distributed among the parties before starting to look for new solutions. 'Let us share the amount saved so that you get 60 per cent and we, as suppliers, settle for 40 per cent'.

- Try to find a distribution scale which both parties consider fair. The gain is distributed in relation to the parties' work effort, costs or risk. Experience, however, shows that the assessment of your own and the opponent's efforts is a sensitive subject. Many negotiations fail because the parties get stuck in an assessment conflict where they seem to have insulted each other by exaggerating their own effort and downgrading the opponent's effort, a conflict which makes the parties' feelings fluctuate and them part as enemies. The opponent who has been entirely impossible, unrealistic, stupid and lacking business maturity gets the blame for the breakdown.

- The parties demand full compensation for their increased costs and exaggerate on their invoices. 'To manufacture and pack the boards in this new way increases our costs from...' Because you focus the arguments on your own effort, you only run a small risk of ending up in an assessment conflict.

- Take advantage of the competitive situation. 'If you buy from us, your total cost will be $20.60 but if you buy the boards from Poland, you will have a total cost of $22.10'. (Of the $6.25 the supplier keeps around $4.30 by raising his price from $3.90 to $8.25.)

- Work towards a prearranged goal. 'If we can present a solution where we have squeezed the costs down from $22.5 today to $20.60, then the order is ours.'

- Try to gain insight into the opponent's calculation. Give him a reasonable compensation for all the increased costs and a modest earning improvement. The rest of the cake is yours.

- Change negotiation method and start fighting. Show the Danish supplier's proposition to the competitor in Poland and tell the Poles how they can improve their competitive situation by starting to deliver in accordance with the newly developed Danish system. This is not a method which we recommend but something which you may encounter in real life if you deal with cheap business relations where the short-term gains are more important than good relations and a good reputation.

How long will our co-operation last?

Can the plasterboard manufacturer in the above example now lean back and earn a lot of money on his new technique? No. The competitors will copy his method. Other building methods and materials will be developed to outsell the plasterboard. The new manufacturing method can be exported to a country with low prices and knock the Danish factory out. A forward-looking producer can himself initiate this development and control it.

He who settles down will have a difficult time on today's open market. No buyer can afford to keep buying in one place because of loyalty.

It becomes more and more difficult to create and maintain competitive advantages. The increased global competition increases the pressure on the companies with respect to rationalization and new development. The good income which previously made it possible for a

> He who settles down will have a difficult time on today's open market. No buyer can afford to keep buying in one place because of loyalty.

company to lean back and be satisfied with distributing the business turnover at 'buffets' with smart negotiation propositions which let to distribution in a zero-sum game is no longer to be found. If the cake which we would all like to get a piece of is going to be big enough for us all, we have to make it bigger first by helping each other.

Exhaustive research

Theorists at the universities as well as the practitioners who live in the 'real' world have time and time again found out that we reach a better common result by means of partnership than if we fight and carry out our negotiation as a zero-sum game. This applies to all negotiations where it is possible to create added value. If on the other hand there is no possibility of creating added value, the zero-sum game is all that remains.

Conclusion and further reading

You are in different ways involved in the changes and negotiations which take place around you. It is your responsibility that they develop in the right way. Whether you see yourself as negotiator, person in charge of change, expert, participant, affected, responsible or spectator, you can influence the development processes in a constructive or destructive way.

In this book you will find many examples, including the one in this chapter on plasterboard. You work with something entirely different. The examples are there to make visible the processes which control us during the changing and negotiating . Why is it a success sometimes? And why do projects which had all the possibilities of becoming a success fail? Where do the different risks lie? How can they be dealt with?

At the end of the book four progressive companies have aimed their sight at the target — partnership. Not just partnership in the sense of the word but also in serious reality. These four companies have in different ways executed a number of processes in order to strengthen their organization and the individual employees' way towards the creation of partnership and the added value.

All four companies have made improvements to their negotiations worth millions of dollars based on this process. But best of all, the gain has not been created at the expense of the opponent. They have made improvements for themselves and for the opponent who read the signal of co-operation, openness, credibility and trust.

Nothing in the four companies' market situation is special or atypical compared to other companies. Everything these five companies have done can be done by other organizations with ambitions, will and abilities.

Through our work and experience with negotiators at all levels and trades we have found that the creation of added values in negotiations in excess of 42 per cent is not unrealistic at all. It often just takes a different approach and will to change. But who would not like to create added value of up to 42 per cent?

What can you learn from the case of the plasterboard? Which similarities do you see to your company? Where do you recognize yourself and your partners? In which connections do the part elements become more important than the whole for you and your partners? Too many people find that the price is always more important than the total costs.

5
This is where we look for added value

If there is motivation, an open mind and enough freedom for individuals in an organization to look for and find new paths, considerable added value can be created if only negotiators know in which direction they are to look. Added value increases the room for negotiation and the cake which can be divided.

The room for negotiation

The traditional room for negotiation can be defined as the difference between the highest price which a buyer is willing to pay, and the lowest price to which a seller is ready to come down. For a deal to be struck, there must be a positive room for negotiation, the buyer must be willing to pay a price above the seller's threshold of pain.

If the maximum price which a buyer can pay is $12,500 and the lowest price to which a seller can come down is $11,900, the difference of $600 constitutes the room for negotiation within which a deal can be struck.

But the actual room for negotiation is normally larger. It consists of the sum of the traditional room for negotiation plus the added value we may create. This allows us to reach an agreement even if the highest price which the buyer can pay is below the lowest price to which the seller can come down.

A simple model to help you locate the added value

Good preparation is extremely important in your search for added value. Very often we see negotiators making the following preparations when making an offer:

> **The Offer**
>
> - **How are we going to submit and explain our offer?**
> - **What questions and objections are the other party likely to put forward?**
> - **What terms, conditions and price should we open with?**
> - **Where is the pain threshold?**
>
> If your opening price is $118,000 and the pain threshold is $103,000 then the room for negotiation is $15,000.
>
> The aim of the negotiation is often defined as: The point is to get the deal, but at the same time we should give away as little as possible of the $15,000.

If you formulate your objective in this manner, you see the negotiation in a much too narrow perspective and you risk finding yourself in a zero-sum game. The last thing you should do as a seller is to give away money in return for getting a deal. If you reduce your price by $5,000, you reduce your profits by $5,000, and the other party makes a deal which is $5,000 better than the original deal. The effect is as 1:1.

You should learn to view the negotiation from a broader perspective. You should do so when preparing so that you are ready for future bargaining.

The four-step model

1. **Our offer.** We have a room for manoeuvre of $15,000. The central question to ask ourselves is 'How can we spend the money rather than lower our price?'
2. **What else have we got to offer, other than money?** What can we add to our offer by way of extra services and products?
3. **Can we reduce the scope of the package?** Which services and products can we take out of the deal? What are the elements that the other party can do for himself? Is there a simpler solution?

4. **The ultimate way out if the other party is not interested in more nor in less:**

    - Try to get something by giving away money, but try to aim for a compromise.
    - Make sure you get a counter offer. You want $118,000, the customer is offering $88,000.
    - If you split the difference, you will land on $103,000. This is the customer's likely objective.
    - Split the difference once again, and you will land on $110,500. This is the customer's likely pain threshold.
    - Place your offer at $107,500 and see how he reacts.
    - If you do not follow this model, but start with cautious one-sided concessions moving down to $115,000, there is a serious risk that you will have to go on making concessions until you reach the bottom.

    The smart thing about providing extra services or products is that the costs to you associated with this may be considerably lower than their value to the other party. In other words, you are getting leverage. The effect might even be high enough for you to raise your price.

    Let us imagine a negotiation in which the buyer receives an offer for ten computers with the software included. The software is to be installed and the computers are to be delivered to the customer's premises. The asking price of the seller for this package is $18,000. The buyer has obtained an alternative offer for similar computers and demands that the seller must reduce his price to a little under $10,000. The seller's pain threshold is $13,000.

    Instead of attempting to accommodate the buyer's demands through a unilateral price reduction to see if the difference can be split around $11,000, the seller asks himself 'What services and products can we add to the package?' If we offer the customer training for five of his staff in Word for Windows, one of the programmes in the software package the customer is buying, what would that mean for us? We hold courses every week, and the standard price for these courses is $450 per person. However, usually one or two places will be vacant in any one course. If we offer these surplus places to the customer, it will not cost us anything.

The seller tells the customer that if there are free places on a course, he can send two of his employees on the course each week. The offer is good for five people. These five participants will get a discount of 50 per cent on the ordinary course fee. If the customer does not think the offer is good enough, the number of people who can participate on these terms can be raised, or the discount can be raised. As an alternative, the seller can offer to supply bigger screens or other types of hardware upgrading at discount prices.

If the customer does not perceive this as providing him with any added value, he is not likely to be interested in increasing the package and get as much as possible for his money. If this is a customer who would rather buy at the lowest possible price, the seller will have to see if he can reduce the package. If the customer himself installs the programmes and collects the computers at the seller's premises, the seller can save $4,000 in working costs. If the buyer takes over these jobs, he can be offered a reduction of $3,000. The seller attempts to hold on to $1,000 to bolster his own net profit on the transaction. If the customer does not bite, the seller can suggest to the customer that if he pays cash in advance instead of getting 30 days' credit, he can get a price reduction and one which is somewhat lower than the interest gain achieved by the seller.

If this does not work, all that is left is haggling. But at least try to take the advice in step 4.

Now you can find added value

In a project there will be many areas in which you can look for added value. Why does it look the way it does? What could be done differently? What would the outcome be?

- Follow the entire process from the birth of the idea to the time when the end user can no longer benefit from the product. Who can do what in the course of this long chain?
- Financial variables and conditions.
- Quality and performance, technical specification of requirements.
- Economies of scale.
- Time.

- Purchasing patterns.
- Rights.

Follow the entire process
'from ear of corn to loaf of bread'

Many years ago the film *From ear of corn to loaf of bread* was produced. Step by step we could follow the lengthy chain that starts with the farmer ploughing his field, and ends when we leave the bakery shop with the newly baked loaf under our arm. Many hands were involved along the path. The film provided a good impression of the entire process.

Carefully follow the courses of events that you embark upon from beginning to end, and ask yourself, 'Why are we doing this? What could we be doing instead? What would be the outcome? Can responsibilities be shared differently? Will this make things better or worse? Where are the opportunities and risks? Can you see something no-one has seen before?'

Start by getting an overview of the current situation. Make a sketch of your findings. The overview is necessary for the pieces to fall into place, and for you to be able to see the whole picture. This picture is the point of departure with which all conceivable modifications should be compared. Often it is necessary physically to follow events step by step to see what is happening, and for every step to ask yourself the following questions.

- Why do they do things this way? Never accept the answers, 'That's how we've always done it', 'That's normal practice in the industry', 'We just follow our routines', 'It works'.
- What will happen when the need no longer exists and the production or the service is to be abandoned? Will the machine be scrapped? Can its life be prolonged? Can it be sold off? Is the system flexible and can it be extended and modernized?
- How does it work today What are the individual elements? How do they affect costs, risks, and profits? How do they affect time, reliability, and useful life?
- Define the factors that have a negative impact on time, costs, reliability, and useful life.

- What could we do instead? What would happen in that case? Positive or negative change? Where are the opportunities and risks and problems? Compare these to the point of departure.

- Who will do the work that has to be done? The most cost-effective party, the one who will benefit most from the experience gleaned, the most risk-orientated party who can sustain adversity. How do we solve the problem if it becomes necessary to transfer the responsibility; do we need to redesign the product, or will anyone require extra training?

- What advantages can new technology provide us with? The emergence of the internet as a channel of information and distribution is an example of new technology that opens up new opportunities and which constitutes a threat to much traditional commerce.

From public authority to commercial enterprise

Do you remember when most householders had only one single telephone point and one telephone often placed in an impractical spot, which made telephoning inconvenient. Ordering a new telephone point and getting it installed took a long time and was very costly. First, the order had to be received and taken down in writing. Then it had to be forwarded to the appropriate district. When a sufficient number of orders had been received by a given district, the supervisor would divide the work up among a number of telephone fitters. The fitter then phoned the customer to set up an appointment. This process took weeks.

The customer was waiting at home for the fitter who had promised to arrive 'some time during the day'. Instead of going to work, you had to put up with sitting around waiting. The fitter generally completed the job in around 30 minutes. He would write out a work report, which formed the basis of the invoice to the customer. The customer thought it too expensive, he would ring the company to complain — but to no avail. This whole procedure very likely cost the company more than the fitting charge and created many dissatisfied customers.

It goes without saying that the telephone company had forbidden customers from installing their own telephone points. We might make mistakes, and the telephone network used electricity. This was certainly not something a layman should fiddle with.

The telephone company earned most of its income from telephony, the easier it was to make telephone calls, the more we would use the phone. But no-one used this approach or saw the connection.

Today in the tele-stores we can buy all the necessary equipment to install as many telephone points as we like. It costs less than $15, and we don't have to worry about how to fit the bits together. A creative technician has invented a connecting plug through which we can connect ourselves to the telephone net. At the same time the monopoly in telephone sales was abolished. We could now buy as many phones as we wanted. It took a long time to transform the company from being a public authority into being a business concern.

Buying a table

Let us try to follow a process that we are able to imagine — buying a coffee table. But we have to go back to the late 1950s. Consider the following example. It shows you how things were done.

1. **I need a new table and go to the furniture store.** Where were all the furniture stores located in the 1950s? In the city centre.

    Advantages: It was easy for customers to get there, and all the stores were in one place. This made it easier to compare products and prices.

    Disadvantages: The furniture stores had to pay very high rents. To make financial sense of things, selling prices were high, and stores could not afford to carry large stocks of finished furniture. Instead they had displays where customers could choose and compare tables manufactured by different factories. This led to long delivery times.

2. **I make my decision, and the order is written out.** Once my choice was made, the order was written out, and I paid a deposit. I was told that the time of delivery would be at least five weeks. The store would send on the order to the factory.

Advantages: A down payment made by customers served to finance some of the furniture store's activities. The store never ran any risk of being stuck with large stocks of unsold products.

Disadvantages: It took an awfully long time. Information of delivery times was often incorrect, which caused a great deal of irritation. The seller would contact the factory to speed things up and to get the new delivery times.

3. **The factory books an order for a table.** As it was not worthwhile manufacturing one table at a time, and if the factory did not have a finished table on stock, it waited until such a time as it could manufacture a short series of a 1950s table.

   Advantages: The factory did not have to invest in costly stocks of finished tables, and did not risk being left carrying a lot of unsold tables.

   Disadvantages: Short production runs and low stocks made it difficult to use advanced machinery, there was a lot of craftsmanship and short series. The evolution of new materials was held back. In part, this explains why the table was so expensive.

4. **The table is transported to the furniture store.** Since it was a matter of an expensive table and long transportation, in the course of which the table had to be transshipped a few times, it was important to use packaging that would protect the table from getting to any harm. To keep down transport costs, attempts were made to group as many items as possible into the same shipment.

   Disadvantage: Groupage took a long time. The alternative was costly: shipping one table directly to the end user.

5. **The table arrives in the furniture store.** The store would check to see if it was, in fact, the correct table, they would phone the customer and make an appointment for delivering the table, which they would then deliver in their own van. The service included carrying the table into the customer's living room, it would be polished, and they would take the packaging material with them when they left. After eight weeks or so I finally had my coffee table and paid the balance of the price to the store.

   Advantages: High service level.

   Disadvantage: Costly handling.

What was in the cartons?

We would like to ask you a question, a question which few people can answer correctly. What was in the carton coming all the way from the furniture factory to my home?

The answer most people give is 'a table'. Indeed, there was a table in the carton, but 90 per cent space in the carton was taken up by air. It is very costly to package, transport, and stock air. The creative individual who originally realized this, approached the party whom we have at the other end of this chain — the designer. He was assigned with the task of designing a table which could be packaged in a box in which no air was included.

The solution was several hundred years old, but had probably been forgotten. British army officers had something constructed that they referred to as a 'campaign table'. This was a collapsible dining table that they could take with them into the field, and which would seat 20 people around it. The legs were detachable, they could be screwed into the table. The table top, which could be folded in the middle, constituted the flat and robust package into which the whole table with detachable extensions and legs could be packaged and transported.

The first furniture designers to be approached would probably have replied: 'Sorry, it can't be done.' They only saw the problems. A table always has a number of legs, so naturally there will always be a lot of air. The legs will have to be fitted to the top at the factory and, consequently, there will always be a lot of air. The legs have to be affixed at the factory, they have to be glued in, not a job that the customers can do for themselves, because they don't have the requisite tools. What was in short supply was creative thinking.

However, a couple of furniture designers had already come up with the solution. The point was not affix the table legs at the factory. Instead this work should be left to the end user. The legs should not be glued on, they should be screwed on. Apparently IKEA trusted those furniture designers and the foundation of the multi-billion company, IKEA, had been cast.

By 2001 the founder of IKEA, Mr. Ingvar Kamprad had an estimated fortune of more than $37 billion.

This change in construction that was developed and made commercially viable by IKEA changed life for an entire industry. It entailed a great deal of added value.

Advantages

- The factory can get around an entire manufacturing element thus reducing manufacturing costs. Today the work and responsibility involved in fitting the table legs rest with the end customer. You buy a table at $225, and you yourself have to affix the four legs. How much do you add to the price by way of compensating you for your work? Nothing. You set the value of your own work at $0.
- The tables can be packaged in flat boxes, and 90 per cent of the air can be dispensed with. Costs involved in packaging, stocking, and transporting the table are considerably reduced.
- By moving the furniture store away from an expensive address at the city centre and to the periphery of the city, the store manages to reduce rent to a level that makes it financially interesting to carry the finished tables on stock. A furniture giant has been born.
- Costumers can take their newly purchased table with them on the same day, and will not have to wait for it for several months. Availability increases notably which, in turn, leads to more decisions to buy and thus to larger turnover volumes.
- The table is packaged so as to allow customers to transport it themselves. The costs connected to the store's furniture van have disappeared.
- The furniture giant does not place an order for a table one at a time, it places orders for 10,000 tables at a time. This allows rationalization of production, the deployment of modern machines, and a more efficient purchasing of raw materials.
- The furniture giant and various factories begin working together to develop better machines and materials. The furniture giant begins transferring know-how between factories.
- The furniture giant has established its activities in Sweden; these have been tested, developed, and routines have been evolved. This activity it can begin exporting to the whole world.

- The welfare state can start furnishing people's homes with good-quality furniture at reasonable prices.

  Disadvantages

- My coffee table can be seen in thousands of other homes.
- From time to time quality has been less than terrific, and we have all of us been forced to go back to the furniture giant because a screw was missing.
- Small factories, exclusive design, high quality, and excellent craftsmanship are finding life difficult. Some of them were knocked out, but the ones who managed to innovate are still in the market, and they are flourishing. They have all found their target groups, and have adjusted their undertakings to these groups.
- A dominating player who runs things and dictates conditions to many of its suppliers.

What can we learn from developments in the furniture industry?

As long as we stay in a rut, business will be conducted as so-called zero-sum games. If we wish to make more money through a deal, we have to squeeze some of the other parties in the chain to take upon themselves higher costs, risks, or liabilities.

In this chain some of the links are the designer, the manufacturer, his employees, the owners and other sources of financing, sub-suppliers of machines and raw materials, forwarding agents, packaging suppliers, retailers and end customers. They have not all been involved in negotiating, but one way or another they are all part of the process of change.

This chain of different stakeholders is also found in many other types of enterprise, enterprises in which no major change has taken place for decades. Production takes a long time, time is money, and what is being produced is too expensive. Distribution is inefficient and costs money. Is the key to improved efficiency to transfer responsibility to the customer? Or is it flat pack, low prices, long series, poor quality, production in third-world countries, or are design changes what is needed? The answers are to be found in your own enterprise. You and your colleagues have the necessary knowledge of the industry to know what it takes.

Analyses in keeping with this model have contributed to the development of undertakings in different lines of industry.

Benchmarking — or who can you copy?

The companies that have come the longest way are normally the ones that have been exposed to competition. Study the companies that have been facing tougher demands. No doubt it will be possible to find added value creating ideas in other industries, ideas that you can use both internally and in business relationships with other partners. Do not make the mistake of looking at your part of the enterprise exclusively. It is very important that you follow the whole stream from the idea stage to the time when the product is no longer used, and that you ask yourself the following question: 'How can the other party benefit from this in other contexts?'

Question the division of responsibility between the different partners; in other words find out if unnecessary duplication of effort is taking place.

- Where, along the chain, are costs generated? Which party has the best cost efficiency?
- Where are the risks located? Who is best suited to handle and run risks?
- Does it take long? Who can or how can time factors be reduced?
- Where are gains generated by way of money, experience, and goodwill? Who will benefit most from these gains?

- Are there any superfluous intermediaries? Might e-commerce suit us? How do I set about selling my own house? Who, in addition to the estate agent, can help me?

Below are a number of examples illustrating how enterprises in various lines of industry have found their way to the added value. Perhaps you can find inspiration in some of these examples.

Financial variables and conditions

Price and terms of payment are ingredients of any business transaction. Companies often follow routines and normal practice for the industry without testing to see whether changing the conditions might yield added value. Often negotiators are not even authorized to discuss conditions other than the standard ones. The people who have determined what these standard conditions should be, are rarely present at the negotiating table and, therefore, have little knowledge of what could be achieved by letting their own negotiators have a free hand. Among financial variables we find:

- terms of payment — credits;
- purchasing, leasing, renting, residual value, repurchase, shared ownership, outsourcing;
- pricing;
- splitting up the price on various accounts and types of costs, budgets, taking tax regulations into account;
- currencies, money, goods and services;
- autogiro, frequency of invoicing, mode of payment, credit cards;
- down payment, royalty.

Terms of payment

The following dialogue is not unusual. The seller asks, *'Would you be willing to consider paying an advance?'* The customer replies, *'No, that's out of the question.'* This is a knee-jerk reaction on the part of many buyers. They do not think that the supplier should be given an advance. Granting an advance can only be done if the supplier can document that he will have considerable expenses accruing over the course of the project. And in that case, any advance will have to be attuned to these costs. This is the attitude of about one-third of all buyers we have come across.

'No,' is the wrong answer. The buyer slams the door without knowing what it is he is declining. He does not have enough information to make an appropriate decision. How big an advance is the supplier asking for, and if he gets the advance he is asking for, what is he willing to give in return? It is only when the buyer can see both elements in the equation that he will be able to determine whether any added value can be created by changing the terms of payment.

What is missing is dialogue, openness, and a clear proposal through which you frankly state what you want, and what you can give.

The rule to follow in a negotiation is: If you want something, you must be prepared to show what you would be willing to give in return. One-sided demands will meet with rejection while an offer leads to constructive dialogue. For example, *'Provided we can get an advance of $300,000, we can accommodate you and take on a considerable share of the costs in adapting the system to your wishes.'*

The buyer should be active in charting the potential options. Behind any wish there is a need. Why does the seller need an advance? What is it worth to him? Can we exchange it for something that is more valuable to us? The seller as well as the buyer should be proactive in the way they negotiate. Create a dialogue and ask questions.

- So you would like an advance? How much?
- Why?
- What is your collateral?
- What will you give us, if we let you have this advance?

The seller must learn to express himself unambiguously, for instance, by making a concrete offer which makes it clear what he wants and what he is willing to give.

- If you let us have 30 per cent in advance, we can lower the price by $12,000.
- If you let us have 30 per cent in advance, we can guarantee that you will take delivery of the shipment before summer.

- If you let us have 30 per cent in advance, we can offer you free service for the entire warranty period.

We have to learn that a 'no' in a negotiation does not necessarily mean *'No, under no circumstances.'* No is a knee-jerk reaction for some people. The seller should make sure he gets an explanation for the customer's negative attitude.

- I see that you don't take kindly to the idea of letting us have an advance, why is that?
- On principle we don't grant advances.
- Why is that?
- It's a risk as well as a cost
- If our bank guarantees the advance, would there be any risk involved as far as you can see?
- No, but it would cost us money.
- How much would it cost you to grant us an advance of $100,000?
- Approximately $10,000.
- If, in return, we were to offer you free service, this is something that normally costs about $12,000 a year, would you then be willing to let us have an advance?
- Let me think about it.

This type of constructive dialogue requires openness. If the customer will not reply by indicating a specific amount, it will be difficult for the seller to determine whether an advance is a way forward. Faced with customer silence, many sellers give up.

A better alternative is to send up a trial balloon by making an offer just to see what the reaction is going to be. 'If we can have an advance of $100,000, we can let you have a full year's service in return. Normally that would cost you $12,000. Why don't you think about it?' In making this clear opening, the seller provides the customer with a real chance of looking into and assessing the suggestion.

A result of such openness could also be that the parties catch sight of other opportunities than granting an advance for creating added value.

- Our liquidity situation doesn't make it possible for us to grant you an advance. We are being charged a relatively high interest rate which we would have to be compensated for if we were to let you have an advance.
- How high is the rate of interest you'd have to pay?
- We calculate with 12–13 per cent.
- Then I see another option. We can offer you a 90 days' credit instead of 30 if you can handle the installation of the equipment. I'm sure the credit will be worth more to you than your installation costs.

If you cannot create added value by changing conditions in one respect, you may turn 180 degrees to see what will happen if you move in the opposite direction. Offer longer credit terms instead of the advance originally asked for.

Many undertakings have long-established policies governing activities. Most of the suppliers we have met will only adjust the terms of payment — net cash 10, 20 or 30 days. They never embark on a discussion of any other terms or conditions. Company policy has never been queried. It has been in place for many years, and no-one remembers what the reasons for establishing it really were.

Many negotiators state that they are incapable of calculating the value of alternative terms of payment. Frequently, they do not know what the rate of interest is that they should apply to their calculations. They also have mechanical problems in actually carrying out the calculation. They may, for instance, be incapable of calculating the value of an advance of $100,000 that they will have at their disposal for 15 months, and for which the rate of return is 12 per cent.

$$100,000 \times 12/100 \times 15/12 = 15,000.$$

We have met buyers and project managers in great corporations who claim that, in connection with their investments, they never take any interest losses or gains into consideration. In these companies, annual investment needs are counted in billions of dollars. The money they have had allocated for their project, they can spend whenever they want in the course of the project period. The implication of that is that with investments of that order of magnitude, their companies risk losing realizable added value to the tune of several millions every year.

We have come across negotiators from small and large businesses who admit that they are, in fact, aware that there is a great deal of money to be found in alternative terms of payment, but that, nevertheless, they would never even discuss modifying the terms. The gains accruing from this would end up somewhere else in the accounts so that the project would not benefit from such gains.

The type of situation we have described here is not uncommon. The prerequisite for creating added value by modifying just one condition, i.e. the terms of payment, is there, but the parties do not take advantage of the opportunity. Several problems are associated with this matter, one of them is insufficient communication and negotiation skills.

The parties are looking straight ahead, blinkers effectively prevent them from catching sight of new ideas or thinking along new lines. Individual freedom to act is restricted by others in the organization. Individuals have not learned to negotiate creatively. Principles along the lines of 'suppliers should not receive any advance' and 'who do they think they are, messing with our internal policies?' are all too common. The result is that realizable added value is not exploited.

Organizations wishing to survive and grow must make certain they take better advantage of the potential. Staff competence is to be developed and supported on a continuing basis. Individuals must be given the responsibility and competence to discuss and ask questions about different solutions. On the other hand, it is not always necessary to delegate the decision-making authority concerning which new routes can be accepted. Management should provide guidelines for determining terms of payment keeping in mind the potential added value to be created.

> The parties are looking straight ahead, blinkers effectively prevent them from catching sight of new ideas or thinking along new lines. Individual freedom to act is restricted by others in the organization. Individuals have not learned to negotiate creatively.

Purchasing, leasing, renting, residual value, shared ownership or outsourcing

Is it ownership or use that matters? What is it we need? Do we view the thing as an investment that must be profitable, so that we will get our money back when we sell the object? Is there any enhanced status associated with actual ownership? Is the need permanent or only temporary? Is our requirement spread evenly over the year/day, or is it cyclical?

What are our financial opportunities? Do we have the necessary manpower to maintain the equipment? Where else would we benefit more from deploying our financial and human resources? Are our requirements today the same as they were five years ago?

When the requirement is most urgent, the customer will accept a higher price. Among all the people who have bought a new car this winter, there is a group of people who do not perceive the need for air-conditioning as urgent. Rather than spending $1200 — the price of an air-conditioning system — they spend the money on a holiday. When the temperature inside their car approaches 30 degrees, they really miss air-conditioning, and now they are willing to pay for it. By means of a credit card, they can activate air-conditioning or other types of equipment, that they chose not to have when they bought the car. At an hourly rate of $4–$6 , they consider it to be money well spent to achieve a pleasantly cool temperature. Car manufacturers will soon recoup the costs involved in making air-conditioning standard equipment in all cars. Modern technology makes it possible to sell a lot of extra products and services when the demand is most urgent.

Many questions and answers may be needed before we can make a rational decision about whether to own or to rent. Purchasing, leasing, renting, residual value, shared ownership or outsourcing are familiar concepts to most business people. We are not going into detail concerning their respective advantages and disadvantages. The point is to locate the solution which, at the lowest cost and risk levels, meet our requirements. What were the questions you asked yourselves, and what answers did you arrive at, before you decided how to acquire the different resources?

For many years it was a self-evident truth in our families that we live in our own house. What made us see this as so self-evident? We were governed by conscious and unconscious assessments:

- you feel safe and secure if you own your own home;
- it's good for the kids to grow up in a nice area;
- this is a high-status area;
- should we believe the politicians who tell us that this is a financially lucrative dwelling?;
- a good investment;
- I want to live where I grew up;
- I love working in the garden;
- we get more space in return for the money we pay.

You can extend the list yourself. All these arguments were more or less true 20 years ago but how are things today? The kids have left home. The area is not what it used to be, and clearing snow and mowing the lawn is a pain, our needs and interests could be far better met somewhere else, and having our money tied up in a highly taxed dwelling seems a bad investment compared to other investment alternatives, and compared to all the fun things we could be doing if we made our money do some work before we are too old. This analysis made it clear that we should put the house on the market and start looking for somewhere else to live.

Now the houses are sold, and our lives have entered a new and exciting phase. One of us lives in an owner-occupied flat in central Copenhagen. We also managed to do without the expensive intermediary, the real-estate agent. Now, all we have to do is spend the money.

Just like we have become set in our ways, we have also allowed perma frost to permeate the ground into deeper and deeper layers concerning the way we view many other aspects of ownership and user rights. The prerequisites for creating added value by changing the mode of ownership are there, but we never seem to find them. Are we afraid to review decisions previously made? Why should we perceive of renegotiation as a risk and a conflict rather than as an opportunity?

Imagine that it were possible for you to start over. What are the requirements today? What are your priorities, what do the alternatives look like now? What would making one choice over an other give you?

Pricing

Price may be calculated according to many different principles. It can be fixed or flexible, it can be a maximum price, an orientation price, an incentive in which we share extra costs and profits, and a price can be adjusted by means of indexes.

We live in a culture with fixed prices. Why? Our fear of conflict, our reluctance to haggle, in combination with our poor bargaining skills, are among the explanations. Price is of central importance in most business transactions. Our success and ability are often measured by the price we achieve. Price is unambiguously reflected on the bottom line. Price can be measured.

Price often constitutes the point in a negotiation where the interests of the parties are on a collision course. This is by no means inevitable. It is possible to create added value out of this conflict. We need more information about the way in which the other party views price, and what price means to him to test whether it is possible or not. The word price can mean different things to different people.

- The sum of money which something costs.
- Being able to pay a high price or a low price is prestigious and creates a sense of belonging to a particular group.
- The correct price is related to my budget, the usefulness of something as perceived by me, the alternatives open to me, the cost or effort which the other party must provide to create his product.
- The asking price is an opening offer and, thus, always exorbitant.
- The price the other party accepts gives me cash in hand. Money that I can spend to meet other requirements.
- The price which the other party accepts is a confirmation of my worth.
- I cannot tell what the correct price is until I know what I'm getting for my money.

We do not always have to go to battle over the price level. It may be possible to create added value by first taking the discussion and then agree a method for fixing the price.

Fixed price. It can be difficult to make a correct assessment of contribution in terms of effort, costs, problems and risks. It is more difficult for the buyer than for the supplier to carry out this calculation. The buyer, who is not keen to run any risk, who has had unpleasant experience with open account terms, who must stay within a given budget, or who must be able to compare the costs involved in different alternatives, needs a fixed price. This buyer might well be willing to accept having to pay a risk premium for this fixed price — a risk premium that might exceed what the supplier needs in order to cover himself. With a fixed price there is an incentive for the supplier to be cost efficient to get his calculation to hang together and yield a profit. Without this incentive, many buyers know that the price can be all over the place.

Flexible price. In those situation where uncertainty concerning a project is considerable, fixed prices are impossible. The risk premium can become excessive. Risks may be underestimated, which could lead to future disputes over unforeseen extra costs. It can be difficult to ascertain whether bills are unfairly inflated. Disclosure agreements and entitlement to scrutinize bookkeeping may be a solution. The supplier will be paid for documented costs plus an additional amount for profits and costs. This is the normal method in connection with monopoly transactions.

- The parties may need to 'sell' the deal internally. If a buyer can show that he has been able to keep the 2001 prices to the end of February 2002, he might be able to get in-house support agreeing to let the supplier get the increase he is looking for, from March 2002.

- If our publishers can persuade us to accept a royalty payment of 20 per cent for the first 3000 copies sold of our book, their calculations may fall into place to get approval for the publication. For copies sold over and above the first 3000, there is no problem in setting the royalty percentage at 26.

- Don't overlook the opportunities associated with combining price with the factors of time and volume.

Orientation price in connection with incentives and a division of extra costs and profits. The parties have a shared responsibility for assessing the costs of the project in a concrete manner if they are to bare a share of any unforeseen costs. The parties' common interest in operating in a cost-efficient manner will increase if they can share in the profits. It is important to find the appropriate orientation price and distribution key.

Fixed price linked to an index. Instead of sitting at the negotiating table arguing about who is the most skilful forecaster and who is best at 'guesstimating' price developments, it is possible retroactively to regulate price deviations and project times by means of an index or a followup calculation. It is important to agree the index and the basis value, and whether the index is to apply to all or only some of the costs.

Price on the basis of results. The price will be calculated retroactively, and the supplier will have to pay in relation to the results achieved. This is an un-Nordic method which is often met with suspicion and the words: 'This is not something we can venture into. It means that you might make an unreasonable amount of money on this number of units supplied. No, we must insist on a fixed price.'

- A customer is planning a direct advertising campaign and wants to know what it will cost him. The customer is looking for an overall price or a specified statement of the cost of the individual components of the campaign. The seller comes back with an offer that seems highly unusual to the customer: 'For every response leading to an order being placed within six months, we want $44.' The customer objects, he wants a 'normal' price.

- Instead of looking to see what he himself can gain from the transaction and relate the costs at 350 for each new order to what this is worth, he is fixated on the how much money the other party can make on this price offer. The buyer does not get the point at all which is, of course, that the more money the other party makes, the more he himself will earn! Do not object to this method. Is there any method that can measure results more certainly? Is it the effort and skill of the supplier which affect the result? Try to make a realistic assessment of the result that can be achieved and try to negotiate a distribution key that provides the other party with an incentive strong enough to take a lot of pains.

Price split up on different accounts and types of costs, budgetary years or by taking tax regulations into account. The problem does not have to be total costs over a period of time. Sometimes the problem can be related to the technicalities of bookkeeping, and a redistribution of costs over time or between different accounts can solve it.

What will be the tax implications of redistributing costs? Some costs can be written off right away while others must be written off over a number of years. Some costs are tax deductible while others are not.

The psychological connotations of price. Many buyers focus their interest on the purchasing price. The amount charged to their budget. This amount might be of greater psychological importance to the other party than to you. By allowing the other party to 'win' the price discussion, the *quid pro quo* that you can get in return may more than offset the costs involved in the price reduction.

The Volvo dealer in Sweden who had achieved the highest district per capita number of cars sold a few years ago followed a certain principle. The customer who wants to buy a new car and who is trading in his old car as part of the deal wants to be told that his old car is in good condition, that its trade-in value is high. Instead of following the trade practice of squeezing down the value of the old car by pointing out all its defects, flaws and signs of age that would have to be fixed before the car could be sold again, this dealer offered customers a good trade-in price, and in return he offered low discounts on new cars.

> The problem is that the parties have become too rigid in their ideas, and blinkers prevent them from thinking innovatively. Principles such as "a price must always be fixed", "we never haggle over price", "we must always have a discount", are applied all too frequently.

Currencies – money, goods or services

In which currency should the price be paid? Danish kroner, Euro, US Dollars or sterling? The answer to this question entails risks and opportunities. We can leave it to others to run the exchange risks by means of hedging, or we can keep the chance of earning some money on exchange rate fluctuations. If you are knowledgeable and willing to run a risk, added value can be created.

The price does not necessarily have to be expressed in money terms. What are the opportunities and risks involved in accepting payment in goods or services?

A newly started enterprise will be in much need of consultancy, but will not have a lot of money. You are a consultant with a well-established firm and a sound economy. Why demand payment in money? Make sure you get an option so that, on easy terms, you can get a share of your customer's future profits.

A firm working in the field of direct advertising seems to have provided shoddy work in connection with a campaign. You complain, and the firm offers a refund of $150. This amount is ludicrous. You speak to a lawyer friend of yours who tries to dissuade you from bringing legal action. Experience shows that the burden of proof is difficult to lift, and that the city court prefers settlements to judgments. It might be an alternative to go for compensation in services rather than in money. You want them to let you have 5,000 new addresses from their mailing list free of charge. Something that will not cost them anything, and a solution that means that you can, after all, go on doing business with each other.

Airlines try to get the loyalty of travellers by being generous with bonus points. Not in the form of money, but in the form of air fares nobody wants to pay for. It does not cost them extra to put you in one of the empty seats.

You are in the business of selling packaging machinery for producing food packaging. The other party is short of western currency, but produces high-quality food and has excess production capacity. Accepting payment in the form of finished food products will probably be far more profitable than insisting on payment in currency. The food can then be sold on to one of the big supermarket chains.

Autogiro, frequency of invoicing, mode of payment, credit cards

How exactly will the physical payment be effected? For those who have many but small transactions, handling invoices, payments, and cash will be costly. We have a telephone operator who, over the years, has sent us invoices for tiny amounts. The only party making any money is the post office. Mobile phone companies had a similar problem in relation to many customers, and in the end they invented 'cash cards' where the customer pays an amount in advance he can make phone calls until the money has run out. Other operators have reduced their administrative costs by getting their customers to agree to automatic debiting via some kind of credit card. Our tele-operator is still losing money hand over fist.

Try to explain all the types of added value that were created when the ICA card was launched in Sweden. The ICA is the Swedish equivalent to WalMart. Under this system, the customer deposits an amount with his supermarket.

The customer gets a better rate of interest on his money than the bank is willing to pay, he gets a monthly statement, and he does not have to hold cash available. The ICA gets money below the banks' rate of interest, customer loyalty grows because the card ties the customer to ICA, useful statistical information is obtained, for instance, on the impact of advertising campaigns, and how well different articles sell.

You can use your credit card to get free credit or as a basis for bargaining. It costs a store a percentage to accept card payment. Imagine that you are going to purchase a new TV and video recorder, a purchase to the tune of $1,875. The store accepts several credit cards. Select from among the cards you carry the one that is most costly for the store. If you don't know which one that is, you just have to ask the store owner which one he would prefer and which one he would like to avoid.

The charge payable by the store owner may be as much as $113 if you pay by credit card. Instead, you offer him cash payment if he is willing to give you a discount, not in money, but in goods. You choose a radio at $140. The store owner's wholesale purchasing price is $80 at most. This figure should be compared to the $113 that the credit card company will charge; thus you both make money on the deal. However, this is a zero-sum game you are playing. The government does not get the VAT on the radio, and the credit card company loses it commission. But this need not worry you or the store owner at all, the transaction is perfectly lawful.

Learn to see the opportunities and choose a different mode of payment

Down payments and royalties

Down payment, lump sum payments, and royalty are the usual types of payment for writers and inventors. Why don't more people follow this example? The principle of a guaranteed flat fee plus a result-orientated remuneration is gaining more and more ground.

Example 1

A publishing house wants to publish our books in Sweden. No-one can tell in advance how many copies can be sold. In the course of our talks with the publishing house we repeatedly receive signals that seem to indicate that we are dealing with cautious people, and that costly new projects are not welcome.

While certainly hoping that the book will sell well, they wish to be prudent and keep their investment low. Reluctantly they let themselves be tempted into a discussion about paying a high guaranteed minimum royalty, i.e. a down payment (lump sum) on signature of the contract.

We have great confidence in our book, and the satisfaction of seeing our it on display in bookstores in many countries is even greater. We offer to adjust the book to an international market, if the publishing house can establish contacts with their colleagues in several countries. If the publishing house can help us reach a wider market, we can drop our demand for a lump sum. Gradually backing down from this demand, we hope to be able to increase the per-book royalty payment, thus achieving a much higher return on our book.

Example 2

Your company is competing for the contract on developing an IT system. How do you intend to charge? A fixed price for the entire assignment? A flexible price based on the actual number of hours taken up by developing the system? A low, fixed price plus a flexible payment on the basis of each transaction effected by the customer? Or simply flexible payment on the basis of each sale?

Decisions must be made on a case-by-case basis. How do you view the project and its potential? How costly will it be to develop? Does your financial position permit a postponement of payment until the customer's system is up and running? If not, will you be able, on the strength of the contract, to get a third party to finance the development? What does the bank have to say?

Why not choose a remuneration on the basis of each transaction when your system is used? This is appropriate if the customer is sensitive to the size of development costs, and in those cases where he can debit his end customer for transaction costs. Will a customer perceive of a cost of $1 as prohibitive each time he uses his smart-card to pay for purchases made over the internet? The amount is negligible to the end user, but it will make the developer of the system a multi-millionaire.

Issues to consider

What will your competitors do? What signals have the customer sent? Are they sensitive to the size of development costs? Will the customer be able to debit his end customer for future payments on a transaction-by-transaction basis? If we were the end customer, would we perceive the costs as a deterrent? Every time you use your smart-card linked to your bank account to pay for purchases made over the internet, your account is debited 50 cents. A negligible amount for each end user, but one that will generate a lot of money for someone who piles them up. How much money do you think the supermarket owners earn by charging 25 cents per plastic carrier box? Have you stopped using them?

Can you close the deal by settling for an arrangement according to which you will be entitled to sell the finished product to other customers? If so, should your original customer be entitled to royalty payments on such sales? If so, would your customer be willing to formulate the technical specification requirements in such a way as to facilitate future resale? Much added value can be found in organizing transactions in an unconventional manner.

Learn how to see the opportunities of discussing payment today or tomorrow.

Quality and performance, the technical specification of requirements

The design of the technical specification of requirements not only determine the quality and performance of a product or a system. They also influence costs, times, risks, and useful effects. How should a specification of requirements be perceived — are we talking about non-negotiable demands, or are they merely preferences? What knowledge of existing alternatives does the person who has written the specification of requirements have? How have the priorities been set? What has been intentionally left out? What needs have governed the wording of the specification?

There are many questions requiring an answer before we can understand the thoughts and wishes behind an individual's specification of requirements. Only then can we attempt an unbiased discussion about what the optimal specification of requirements will look like, and what the room for manoeuvre is creating and exploiting added value.

Set out a systematic analysis of all requirements

In order to understand the requirements made, they have to be determined one at a time. A systematic analysis can be carried out according to the following steps and be placed in a matrix as shown below.

Variable	Point of departure	Negotiation arena	Change of conditions

Capacity 100 units/hour

The daily need is 70 units/hour

And you want a bit excess capacity of 80 – 110 units/hour. At 80 units/hour there is a risk of lack of capacity in the peak season. Over the next couple of years you cannot use more than 90 units/hour.

How does the requirement of a capacity over 100/hour affect the chances of the supplier being able to deliver on time and at an acceptable price? How will the requirement impact on maintenance costs and useful life? Are we within the scope of a standard machine or is a special-purpose machine required? Does the supplier have an alternative suggestion?

The answers to all these questions may show that requiring a capacity of over 80 units/hour is unusual. The machine would have to be redesigned. It takes time and money to design a special-purpose machine. Uncertainty and risk are associated with any type of innovation. On the few occasions when a capacity of more than 80 units/hour is required, the customer might solve his problem by operating three shifts instead of two. This would cost far less. In the event that the need for a higher capacity becomes permanent, the machine could be designed so as to allow reconstruction when and if required.

If we are to convince the customer of this solution, it is necessary that we find out how the requirement concerning excess capacity will affect delivery time, costs and the risk always associated with innovation.

If this is to work out in a real-life negotiation, it is necessary for the two parties to trust each other, to have the courage to open up to each other, and to be in possession of sufficient professional expertise to form an overview of both alternatives.

Quality and performance will affect costs during the different phases of the project

The technical specification of requirements is made up of a mixture of requirements that have to be met for the project to work, and of a list of wishes for more or less valuable and interesting functions. For technical reasons, by way of bargaining chips, there might be demands, that you are willing to waive in the course of the negotiation.

The specification of requirements should not be left entirely to operators and technicians. Their reasons for including or deleting certain functions may be of a personal nature rather than in the best interest of the company, functions of which the costs to the company are not in keeping with their useful effect.

Beware of the 'negotiating trap technician-technician', so that they are not allowed to develop new products and systems without taking into accounts the costs, loss of time, and risks. Costs, risks, time consumption, and physical effort must always be related to the useful effect that can be achieved during the different phases:

- development;
- production;
- service and maintenance;
- winding up.

The specification of requirements will influence:

- flexibility, extensibility, and compatibility;
- possibility of selling to several users;
- possibility of extending the useful life of the product;
- reliability and environmental impact;
- useful life;
- user friendliness and working environment.

Many years ago nuclear power stations were built. Everybody knew that nuclear power plants have a limited technical and financial useful life, and that they would have to be taken out of commission some time in the future. The nuclear power plants that are no longer useful have to be demolished. Such an activity is costly as well as risky. What considerations were factored in at the time of designing the plants? Were any options for decommissioning the nuclear power plants in a risk-free manner at low costs built into the project?

Economies of scale

The motivation behind many mergers is the economies of scale that the parties can achieve by spreading out high development costs, production overheads and distribution for a higher number of units produced. However, these gains must be viewed in relation to the changes that will be a consequence of the larger-scale operation.

If, as course providers, we circulate our course catalogue to 10,000 potential customers, there will be high costs involved in locating their addresses and for postage. If we join forces with a colleague who provides another course, (one that is not in competition with ours) we can halve our costs. If we enter into co-operation with a large-scale course provider, who manages several hundred courses every year, someone who has his own mailing list, high postal discounts, and can send out information of five or six courses in the same envelope, costs might end up being only one tenth of the original amount.

> The motivation behind many mergers is the economies of scale that the parties can achieve by spreading out high development costs, production overheads and distribution for a higher number of units produced. However, these gains must be viewed in relation to the changes that will be a consequence of the larger-scale operation.

What are the disadvantages to doing this? Our message may drown in the flood of courses on offer. If the recipient does not think that the first one or two courses sound interesting, he might throw everything into the wastepaper basket. If the recipient dislikes one of the courses on offer, there is a serious risk that he will dislike all the courses. We might even have to put up with all the courses being presented in a uniform format. We might have to accept that everyone who wants to be included in the material must have an identical profile in terms of price and other conditions. Economies of scale can be had at a price, but the price should be in keeping with the concomitant benefits.

When we began writing this book, the business pages of the newspapers were having a lively discussion concerning the merits or otherwise of the mergers planned between Volvo/Scania and Volvo/Ford. One opinion was that a domestic Swedish merger would be preferable, others expressed serious doubts: 'A wholly Swedish solution will constitute a threat against thousands of jobs. In many ways this transaction is comparable to BMW joining Mercedes passenger cars in Germany — a daft notion. The point of mergers is to create added value by locating complementary products, factories, competences, and markets. Scania and Volvo merged will not be able to hold on to their market share, the turnover lost will not be offset by the realizable economies of scale.'

Everyone can believe what they want to believe, and today no-one knows what would have happened. In a few years, we shall know what happened, but we shall never know what would have happened if they had done something else or selected another partner.

Time

Time is one of the critical factors in an agreement. The time most frequently discussed is the time of delivery; how much would earlier delivery cost, how much would we earn by getting started ahead of schedule, what is the cost involved in a delay, and what can we earn if we do not have to accelerate the project? But there are other time aspects for which it is more usual to simply follow established practice rather than taking an unbiased look at different alternatives:

- duration of the agreement;
- the agreement start and expiry dates;
- period of notice;
- winding-up period;
- period of suborders.

Most frame-work and co-operation agreements run for a year, Why? Companies report their results every year, budgets look ahead for a year, there are 12 months to a year, why would we chose another period , *it's practical*, are the replies we usually get. Many co-operative ventures entail risks, costs, and advantages in concluding an agreement for 6 months, 18 months, or 3 years. These matters are not sufficiently discussed and tested.

Most agreements enter into force on 1 January and come to an end on the last day of December. Many of the people responsible for renewing and re-negotiating agreements are faced with a workload in November and December which means that they do not have time to do a proper job. Many partners find it difficult to get a good overview of the following year's conditions until some time into the new year. Nevertheless, they have to commit themselves to an agreement whose terms and consequences they cannot fully appreciate. To protect themselves they add excessive risk premiums to the agreement.

It matters a great deal to the party who has to re-plan his activities whether an agreement is terminated at 6 or 12 months' notice. Short cancellation times can be valuable to another party. Consider the pricing practices of the airlines — you might learn something.

Preparedness costs money. What is the usefulness in practice of a service agreement for a computer system in which the supplier promises to turn up within six hours? Will the system be up and running within six hours? The interesting point is not when the repair man turns up, what matters is when the fault will be remedied. Can you use your old computer instead, or can you borrow a colleague's computer. It might be a good idea to keep your old computer in reserve rather than scrapping it.

How much does the stockbroker lose if his customers cannot complete their deals for a whole day because his internet server is down?

How much is it worth to me having a guaranteed seat on a plane if I confirm the booking six hours before departure? How much can my wholesaler earn, if all orders are to be confirmed no less than a week in advance? Could he perhaps, take on the expenses involved in carrying emergency stocks so that I never risk being left without raw materials?

Purchasing patterns

It is quite possible to make money by filling fruit baskets, refrigerators, watering flowers, tending coffee dispensers, stocking up stores and factories. Managing purchases and making inventories cost money. No-one in the firm wants to be responsible for buying coffee. Others are quite willing to do that job, provided they can make money on doing it.

Modern technology capable of reading bar codes can monitor and govern the entire process. If the customer doesn't have time to make it to the store, the store can make it to the customer. The optician will come to your business on Friday morning and fit out everyone who wants to with new spectacles. It only takes ten minutes instead of taking up an entire lunch break when you really ought to have lunch with a customer. As a channel of commerce and information the internet has created a revolution. Suppliers and customers are only a mouse click away from each other. Buyers and sellers join forces to gain a stronger position and to make their businesses more efficient. Information belongs to everyman and makes for keener competition. Traditional distribution of goods is headed for an early grave.

Rights

In any contract, there are many rights that should be discussed and regulated by the contract terms. Not only does this provide an opportunity of creating added value, it also prevents many future disputes from even arising.

For example, a buyer wants to place a development assignment. He pays for the development and gets a product with which he is satisfied. Will the seller be entitled to sell this or similar products to other customers? Will this right be unrestricted, or is it going to be restricted to certain markets, a specific period, should some customers be excepted, or must it be a full year before anyone else may buy the same product? Is the buyer who paid for the development entitled to some kind of royalty? Will the customer who paid for the development be entitled to a status of most favoured customer, i.e. he will always be entitled to a free upgrading of the system, and nobody else can buy at lower costs than him?

Consider another example. You have written a book; the publishing house asks for an option to have it published in another language and in a different medium. What will you get in return for assigning the rights to someone who has undertaken no obligation? Should you demand that they must spend a certain amount on marketing the book to other publishing houses? Should the option be limited in time? Should you insist on compensation if they do not take up the option within the time limit? Are they going to have any influence over, or perhaps even a right of veto, if they do decide to take up the option? How are you going to divide any profits between you if they can resell your book? Should you insist on a guaranteed fee irrespective of whether they manage to sell the book or not?

Example: Telia and Ericsson

Imagine Telia placing an order with Ericsson for the development of a new mobile phone system. To the buyer this is not a transaction for which they must only discuss the technical specification of requirements, price for the development effort, and price for future service provision. Telia will also have to view the deal from a global perspective and ask itself, what will happen once the deal between us and Ericsson is in place and we have taken delivery of the system ordered?

Obviously Ericsson will wish to sell the newly developed system to other mobile phone operators in Sweden and elsewhere. Who has paid the largest share of the development costs? Who has tested the system in full-scale operation? Who has placed an order for serial production allowing Ericsson to get production going? Telia has.

Have the parties discussed the conditions under which Ericsson would be entitled to sell to other customers, customers who are Telia's competitors, and have they discussed how earnings on such sales will be divided between the parties?

A number of important questions are raised.

- Will Ericsson be allowed to sell to Telia's competitors? Will such transactions only be allowed to take place after a number of months, so that BT can keep its technical lead?

- Should the technical specifications be adjusted so as to be compatible with the networks of other operators from the outset?

- How high a proportion of development costs should fall to Telia and to Ericsson, respectively?

- If Ericsson develops the system further for other customers, should Telia have access to the newest technology? And will Telia get this free of charge?

- Will Telia be given status as 'most favoured customer', i.e. the price that Telia has to pay for the system will always be lower than the price payable by Telia's competitors?

Key concepts to think about are:

- the right to sell;
- the right to produce;
- ownership rights;
- user rights;
- exclusive rights;
- option rights;
- right of veto.

6
Negotiations as zero-sum games or as co-operation

The creation of partnerships and added value are not possible without basic skills in negotiation techniques.

Negotiation methods can be subdivided into two main categories: zero-sum games and co-operation. The question isn't which of the methods is right or wrong, but what combination you should choose to get the best possible result. You use co-operation to build up relationships and trust, and to create added value. In zero-sum games you negotiate about the division of this added value.

The creation of partnerships and added value are not possible without basic skills in negotiation techniques.

Zero-sum games lead to low-quality solutions

In pure zero-sum games the alternatives permitting technical and financial rationalizations are rarely taken advantage of. Zero-sum games often lead to solutions with winners and losers, or solutions in which both parties lose.

In zero-sum games the negotiation often constantly centres round a solution that has been a given from the outset, and what is debated is the distribution of profits, responsibilities and tasks. The discussion is concerned with a cake which is to be divided. The larger the slice that goes to the other party, the less will be left for you. All gain is made at the expense of the other party.

The technique used by negotiators in connection with zero-sum negotiations is very much characterized by bluffing, threatening, and playacting. In various ways they attempt to force the other party to make concessions. But the gains they make cost more than they are worth.

A supplier has demanded that 30 per cent of the price must be paid in advance. This advance is worth $100,000 to him. The buyer claims that none of the other suppliers has asked for an advance, and he goes as far as to add, 'Our policy is not to give any advances. If you demand in advance, the deal is never going to happen.'

The seller, who isn't a very clever negotiator and who has a very rigid framework within which to operate, gives in. The result of this concession is that his costs on the transaction go up by $100,000. How much does the customer gain? Let us assume that his interest costs are somewhat lower than that of the supplier. His gain is then $70,000. In this zero-sum game the parties lose $30,000.

By means of a more skilful negotiation technique, the $100,000 that the seller negotiated away might have been utilized in an alternative manner yielding higher profits for the buyer. A better solution for both parties would have been a unilateral price reduction of $80,000. The seller would have earned another $10,000, and the seller would have saved $20,000.

The seller might even have better alternatives. He might have been able to include one year's free service — a service that might have been more valuable to the customer than better payment conditions.

Unfortunately it's normal for negotiators to work with solutions that are unnecessarily costly in connection with zero-sum games. The resources disappear into thin air and neither party has a share in them. Furthermore, zero-sum games lead to a negative negotiation climate in which the parties demonstrate mutual lack of trust and openness.

Lack of openness means that when the negotiators are deciding on the terms which they will ask for, or which they are willing to accept, will only look at the consequences to themselves. They do not have, nor have they attempted to obtain, information about the consequences of the terms and conditions to the other party. The decision leads to sub-optimization. The existing possibilities for rationalization and optimal distribution of costs aren't taken advantage of.

Other sellers facing demands usually become more defensive when they come under pressure. They don't believe the buyer's gambit that the competitors haven't asked for an advance. They put up counter arguments such as 'Today everybody asks for an advance' 'if we don't get an advance, we have to raise our prices' 'so far, you've always accepted paying an advance.'

A typical solution to this type of verbal combat is a reduction of the advance from 30 per cent to between 10–20 per cent. Thus, the parties have a loss to share, albeit a smaller one. They are stuck in a pattern which will govern their continuing negotiations. Argument is used to counter argument, and a tough attitude will be mixed in with slick, tactical moves. Negotiations now seem like a poker game, and gradually neither party can tell if the other is telling the truth or not.

Don't view the demands with which you're faced as threats. Behind them you might find opportunities that can yield added value if appropriately utilized. To find out whether this is the case, you must use a different technique from resistance. You need to get the constructive dialogue going.

Co-operation means a bigger stake

A systematic search for added value may yield new solutions that can more easily meet the requirements of both parties. If they have a bigger cake to share between them, it's more likely that they will be able to find a division that is acceptable to both. This may lead to the creation of a partnership in which two satisfied parties need not relinquish any need to arrive at a sound businesslike agreement. Equal success, not achieved at the expense of one of the parties as is the case in a zero-sum game.

> Negotiating means carrying out an unbiased review of the existing alternatives.

Negotiating means carrying out an unbiased review of the existing alternatives. If you want to find better solutions than those already at hand, or if you want to obtain extra information about the requirements made, you should use a different negotiation method — the one I refer to as co-operation/partnership. It's characterized by constructive dialogue. The foundation for such co-operation is trust and openness.

In the case in point the seller could reply 'The interest gain we'd obtain against the advance will benefit you by way of a lower price. We can certainly look at the financing aspects and the amount of the advance, but that will affect the price.'

The seller has left the way open for a discussion. The buyer listens and asks 'How much is the advance worth to you?' Now the need for openness and honesty arises. Will the seller be open and honest and reply 'Around $100,000'? In that case the buyer knows how cost intensive his demand is, and he can relate the extra cost of $100,000 to his gain of $70,000. He can see that it eats up more than it yields, and he can try to find out whether other requirements would give a better yield. He sees the opportunity and exploits the difference between the interest costs of the two parties, and instead he offers a higher advance if he gets a share of the added value thus accruing. 'We can raise the advance by 50 per cent, but then you have to come down by ...'.

Co-operation makes serious demands on the negotiators

It's difficult for most negotiators to get well-functioning co-operation going. They have insufficient insight into the advantages that can be realized, and they aren't very motivated to look for co-operation. They are not aware of the demands with which the method faces them and their negotiation partners. They don't have the ability to get the open and constructive dialogue going, and this is an unqualified precondition for getting co-operation to work.

The ability to be rational is restricted if and when they are emotionally affected by the negotiations. Threats, insecurity, and stress are countered with fight or flight — a knee-jerk reaction.

Subconscious wishes and motives

Usually we don't have insight into our own conscious and subconscious needs and desires, and this leads to conflicts that we attribute to the other party. Without being conscious of it we are led into situations where our subconscious actions engender conflicts. Only when we have become aware of these mechanisms and have learned to see the connection between our conscious and our subconscious action, will we attain the maturity required to tackle certain types of co-operation.

A woman is cooking dinner when she discovers that she has forgotten to buy cream. She asks her husband, who is watching sports on the TV, to go down to the service station to buy some cream. Her husband doesn't really want to leave his comfortable chair. He now faces an internal conflict as he also wants to meets his wife's wishes. He is really a 'nice' man who does everything to avoid conflicts, or postpone them.

The service station is five minutes away on foot, but it takes a full hour before the husband is back. His wife is very annoyed and asks:

> "But where have you been? I've been waiting and waiting, and our dinner is all but ruined."

> "First I went to the service station, but they wanted $1.50 for the cream. I know that it's only $1 in WalMart."

> "So you walked all the way to WalMart, another three kilometres to save 50 cents!"

> "I don't think it's fair the way they try to take advantage of the customers at the service station."

> "I'm sure you only did it to annoy me. You were cross because I made you leave your television, but you're always too cowardly tell me straight out!"

Does the husband realize that he did what he did to get even with his wife? He may not be willing to admit to his motive and deny his wife's assertion. He feels he is being treated unfairly. He did sacrifice his TV programme to go and get the cream his wife had forgotten to buy.

He must learn to live with ungratefulness and trouble until he learns how to face conflicts, and be more conscious of how he is governed by subconscious motives and needs.

We aren't rational, not when we negotiate, nor when we make decisions. (I see decisions as negotiations we have with ourselves.) Although most of us try to stand on firm ground, collect and assess facts, there are always subconscious and repressed needs, motives, fears, and hopes in the background. We are governed by them. It's important to be aware of these subconscious needs. The goal is to become aware of our own desires, intentions, and emotions in each situation — to lower our defences so that we become conscious of our impulses and will know how to control them.

If you yourself don't have sufficient insight in how your behaviour, choice of route, language, and ability to communicate vary and are governed in different situations, how then could the other party across the table be able to understand, predict, and react correctly to your signals and decisions? In the field of negotiation technique there is no such thing as the absolute truth, nor is there any list of correct results in which two plus two will always make four.

You should acquire several methods and view them as the strings on a guitar on which you can combine an infinite number of chords. You should train your musical ear and become responsive so that resonance can arise between you and the other members of the orchestra.

Your choice of strategy and tactics is one of the most important points for you when preparing to negotiate. If strategy and tactics have not been thought out, you leave the initiative to the other party and will be forced to negotiate on his terms and conditions.

Choice of strategy

Your choice of strategy and tactics is one of the most important points for you when preparing to negotiate. If strategy and tactics have not been thought out, you leave the initiative to the other party and will be forced to negotiate on his terms and conditions.

The strategy is the philosophy according to which you work, and it impacts on your behaviour during negotiation. Tactics are those moves, ploys, and stratagems you make use of in the negotiation.

Most negotiators have never really planned any strategy. They adjust their behaviour to the moment, and they change their strategy in a poorly planned manner in the course of the negotiations.

The example of the ten oranges

By way of conclusion, the following allegory can be used to illustrate the five strategies of negotiation:

- combat;
- concession;
- stalling;
- compromise;
- co-operation.

In a room there are ten oranges in a bowl. In two adjacent rooms there at two groups who assign their negotiators with the task of collecting the ten oranges.

The negotiators enter the room at the same time and discover that they've been assigned with the same task, but there aren't enough oranges for both of them. They're facing a conflict.

Combat

If they chose combat, threats and harsh words will soon be heard. Verbal combat may turn into physical combat. None of them feels certain that he'll win, nor can they be sure about how the group will like a victory won through combat. Therefore, both negotiators relinquish combat.

Concession

Concession means that they escape from conflict and leave all the oranges to the other party. The loss of prestige vis-à-vis the group will be highly unpleasant, and the negotiators won't relinquish their personal needs to achieve a good negotiation result. Therefore both negotiators relinquish concession.

Stalling

Stalling will mean that they'll leave the room together to go and have coffee. Maybe, one way or another, the problem will solve itself. Your own group might give you new directives, or maybe the other party will cave in. Negotiation doesn't change the situation. The conflict is still there. If they take advantage of the stalling to try to obtain more information, this might be a way ahead.

Compromise

Compromise will mean a division of the ten oranges. But you want more than five for yourself. Then it becomes easier to motivate the compromise to yourself and your group. Now it's important to have clever arguments. Perhaps you tell the other party 'Yesterday you took all the oranges. You have already received what's due to you. But I'll be a nice guy and let you have two.'

Later on, two may become three or possibly four. The other party also knows how to argue, and consequently he says 'It's quite true that we took them all yesterday. You didn't want any. If you had wanted the oranges today, you should have said so then. Naturally these belong to us.'

The compromise doesn't lead to any solution which is acceptable to the negotiators in this case. None of them wants to look a loser. Both of them want more than five oranges each.

Co-operation

Co-operation means that together they try to solve the problem. But before they can do so, more information is required. When are the oranges to be used, and what are they going to be used for? The two negotiators don't know, and they decide to ask their groups. Later on they meet again in the room. The oranges are to be used immediately. One group needs the oranges for juice, the other for marmalade. Now the solution seems clear to them: first one group will squeeze the juice out of the oranges and then they'll give the bowl to the other group who can now prepare their marmalade.

By frankly informing each other they established that their needs weren't contradictory, and that both parties could have their needs met. Both parties can feel like winners. (According to the experts, however, the marmalade will taste better if the juice is included.)

One precondition for the negotiation to start functioning and solving the conflict with which the negotiators were faced, was the fact that the communication — which from the outset had been one-way only — became two-way. As long as the negotiators are inclined to argue and manipulate each other, the pieces of the jigsaw puzzle that are necessary for an optimal resolution of the conflict won't be revealed.

When communication becomes two-way, the questions are asked and the answers provided, that will allow the negotiators to find completely new solutions to the conflict.

Your choice of strategy permeates the negotiation and determines the negotiation climate. It influences your relations with the other party. Your choice of strategy also influences the signals you receive from the other party, your perception and interpretation of the negotiation, and your personality. It is a result of your upbringing and your heredity. The behaviour you demonstrate in a business negotiation is often very much in keeping with your behaviour vis-à-vis your family members, your neighbours and colleagues.

Your choice of strategy is often affected by your expectations regarding a negotiation. If you believe that the other party will be quite aggressive and spoiling for a fight, you will yourself favour a fight without first examining whether another strategy would be better suited to the purpose, or if a fight will in fact take you to your goal.

If the other party appears to be willing to co-operate, you yourself will tend to be co-operative. If you register aggressive signals from the other party, you will spontaneously respond aggressively. In negotiations there is a law of nature stating that pressure engenders counter pressure.

The organization's policy and general view of the surrounding world will affect your choice of strategy. The negotiator will adjust his behaviour to what he thinks the organization and its managers expect.

Some negotiators are aware of the importance of their choice of strategy — they very consciously plan a strategy and how to implement it. They always take into account the topical negotiation situation and have learned how to vary their strategy and how to switch between different existing strategies. They see the negotiation in two steps: to create and to divide added value.

Their behaviour at the negotiating table is governed by goal-oriented planning and by a feeling of how their own behaviour and reactions to the other party's moves bring them closer to their objective. They have developed their register of emotions, and are sensitive to human interaction. They avoid all types of verbal combat, provocation, locks, and prestige-oriented conflicts that aren't part and parcel of a conscious set-up for the negotiation.

There is no such thing as a general tactic that will work no matter what the circumstances. Tactics will always have to be adjusted and adapted to your objectives, the strategy of your choice, your own resources, your knowledge and the objectives, strategy, resources, and knowledge of the other party.

There is no such thing as a general tactic that will work no matter what the circumstances.

Some tactics are constructive and lead to greater openness and better understanding. They create trust. Using them will make it easier for you to find the paths that can lead you to the added value. However, much of the tactical play aims at manipulating the other party, at making him insecure, and at exerting pressure that may become overwhelming and make him give in. These stressful moves may be efficient in the short term, however, they tend to ruin relationships, trust, and openness. There are negotiation situations in which co-operation between the parties work well so that all tactical, clever moves are superfluous and do more harm than good.

Sometimes it's difficult to determine in advance whether one tactic is superior to another, or whether clever gambits and moves do more harm than good. Only when negotiations have been completed will you know the outcome. But you never know what the outcome would have been if instead you had chosen another strategy.

A good principle in your choice of tactics is to begin with gambits that don't lock the negotiations by limiting the possibility of choosing different routes at a later stage. Try to design the negotiations with a view to co-operation from the outset. If you're uncertain about the intentions of the other party, you should take it easy and wait until you think you can read them. Be wary of using any gambits yourself that the other party might interpret as combative. Such gambits may easily lead to negotiations being deadlocked and preempt future co-operation.

Tactical moves must be made with good sense and caution. Clever tactics tend to be two-edged swords. If the other party sees through your intentions, a clever countermove may still put him where you want him. Negotiations are reminiscent of chess. Just like the chess player, the skilful negotiator is always some moves ahead of his opponent.

Never use a tactic without making clear to yourself what reactions and countermoves this might provoke on the part of the other party, and how you intend to handle these responses. Put yourself in his shoes, and consider how you yourself would have reacted to your gambits, and what your own countermoves would have been. In this way you can see whether you're about to ruin relations and openness before it's too late.

When you're testing boundaries and positions, you should evince firmness, stick to your guns, and motivate your demands. You should learn to do so without reverting to combative moves.

It's the rule rather than the exception that negotiations are full of surprises. It always becomes clear that the picture you had of the negotiation was incomplete and partially wrong. You must be responsive and flexible so that you can adjust to the reality that you come across at the negotiating table. Unfortunately many negotiators are inflexible, and instead they try to force reality to adjust to their negotiation as they have designed it.

> If negotiations are slipping from your grip: take a break!

Keep in mind that my assessment of behaviour at the negotiating table and choice of strategy and tactics isn't shared by everybody. I'm a staunch believer in co-operation. Co-operation is based on trust and open and honest communication between the parties together with a willingness to listen and understand each other's needs and judgements. Co-operation in no way means shirking the issues or relinquishing your own needs and judgements. The purpose is to make the stake as large as possible, to the benefit of both parties.

How the combative negotiator chooses his strategy

There are many negotiators with different ideas about how to structure a negotiation. To them combat is a matter of course; they take a different view of the value of solutions with two winners, and of ethics and morality.

In such negotiations you shouldn't let yourself be hampered by your principles. You have to play the game. This is why it's important that as a negotiator you're familiar with the methods that you yourself consider fair as well as those that you view as unfair.

You shouldn't embark on a negotiation with the kind of tactical gambits that you consider to be morally reprehensible. But if the other party does, you must know how his tactics work, what he hopes to achieve, and how you can neutralize his moves. This is why you will find a number of tactical moves in this book, moves that I myself consider reprehensible.

'Trust is good, control is better', is an old Russian saying. This maxim very much permeated the view taken on negotiations and choice of strategy that typified the former Soviet system.

The difference between trust and control isn't just a question of hidden microphones and unfair methods. In negotiations based on an adversarial philosophy, trust is not required.

From the point of view of the Kremlin, combat was perceived as an excellent strategy. If the other party was accommodating and reasonable this only encouraged the Soviet negotiators to pursue the fight.

According to the Soviet mentality and philosophy you withdraw if you encounter serious opposition. If you encounter someone with a reasonable attitude, you exploit the situation to your own advantage. This behaviour shows how dangerous it is to make unilateral concessions. The attitude was, according to Arkadij Sjevtjenko, UN ambassador and vice-secretary general of the UN, fundamental to Soviet behaviour in connection with negotiations.

I'll leave any moral judgement to my reader. Remember that an agreement concluded between two satisfied parties will always be the best agreement in the long run. Unfair methods are shortsighted. If you hoodwink the other party, you're going to pay for it sooner or later.

When choosing your strategy and tactic, you should adapt to the norms of the market in which you find yourself. For example, a high degree of morality based on Danish norms and values may constitute a handicap in many international contexts. Danes are often naive, gullible, and behave like nice guys in markets where greater toughness is required,

Learn to be mild in manner, firm in substance
suaviter in modo, fortiter in re.
The objective is to get as much as possible from the negotiation
without being perceived as a combative negotiator.

Five different types of behaviour

Human beings were made to survive in a tough world. Aggressiveness has been a precondition for survival, and nature has made a selection in which the strongest survived. Combative behaviour as the natural and only appropriate mode has been left to us as a legacy for generations. Only too rarely has it been queried.

As discussed earlier in this chapter, the different methods of negotiation can be categorized under the headings combat, concession, stalling, compromise, and co-operation.

Combat may arise in many ways. There is the combat in which the negotiator clearly shows his intentions through an aggressive type of communication, threats, and lack of interest in listening to the other party. There is the combat in which the other party does listen and behaves unassumingly to give the impression that he wants to understand the other party while, at the same time, hiding his intentions with the negotiation. Before he shows his true colours, he has made sure that you've already revealed too much.

During one and the same negotiation, you change your behaviour. The method I come across all too often is the ill-planned and unintentional mix of combat, concession, stalling, and compromise. These negotiators are all too frequently characterized by mistrust, aggressiveness, and aloofness — a method of negotiation that leaves only two options: short-term victory or defeat.

Behavioural changes are, as a rule, neither planned nor intentional. Sometimes — but far from always — they can be anticipated. You let yourself be carried away by the negotiation and be controlled by the other party's signals. Gradually you move away from rational behaviour and start reacting more and more emotionally. Thus you lose your ability to control and steer the negotiation in an appropriate direction.

Many negotiations can be compared to a ketchup bottle: At first nothing happens – the negotiations are like a viscous substance, and nobody dares take the initiative. After a while the parties have become involved in verbal combat over an unimportant and not very touchy issue that will only very marginally affect the end result. Time passes until someone realizes that things will have to be speeded up. All the essential issues are now settled within a such a short time that the parties fail to gain an overview of their negotiating position. The agreement is forced through, and opinions of what's been agreed differ, not just between the parties, but also internally in the negotiation delegations.

Increased awareness of the mechanisms that govern your behaviour and that of the other party and switching between negotiating methods is therefore necessary if you want to learn how to steer the negotiations towards the goals you have set yourself.

One and the same negotiation is perceived differently

When a negotiation method and the result it leads to are to be assessed this is always done on the basis of different viewpoints. Our perception of the negotiation differs. Was it effected by means of combat or co-operation, was the result good or bad, did the negotiators signal weakness or diffidence, or did they display strength?

Depending on who we are, and on the perspective from which we view the negotiations, we'll arrive at different, and sometimes entirely contradictory, assessments of one and the same negotiation.

You should view the negotiation and the play surrounding it from a multidimensional perspective, and not let yourself be fooled by simplistic and one-dimensional explanatory models, in which one behaviour is always right, and others always wrong.

Consider the following scenario. Three people enter the same room. On leaving the room, they must describe what they've seen. Number one describes the size of the room, its furniture and colours, and mentions that the owner must have good taste.

Number two perceives his stay in the room as unpleasant. He describes the atmosphere between the people in the room as hard and artificial. He feels that the room is full of tension, that a conflict was about to break out.

Number three lyrically describes a painting by a famous artist that he had seen on one of the walls. All the descriptions are correct, but none is complete. The reality we see and describe provides a revealing picture of ourselves as an individual. In science this method is used to diagnose people.

No-one can claim that his description, assessment, and interpretation of a negotiation is more correct than somebody else's. All interpretations may be correct and truthful when viewed from a certain perspective. Correct perspective is not synonymous with your own perspective. You have no right of interpretation over and above other people. One of the greatest problems pertaining to negotiation is that we arrive at the negotiating table with different maps. Spend time and energy on endeavouring to understand the map the other party has in front of him.

> You should view the negotiation from a multidimensional perspective, and not let yourself be fooled by simplistic and one-dimensional explanatory models, in which one behaviour is always right, and others always wrong.

You should view the negotiation from the perspective of the other party, then you'll learn to understand how the other party functions. This, in combination with insight into your own behaviour, may lead you to successful negotiation. A negotiation in which both parties' needs are met, and their value as human beings is confirmed. A negotiation in which both parties will follow up on what they've undertaken and live up to the spirit of the agreement.

If you limit yourself to viewing the negotiation from your own perspective, things might easily go wrong. One negotiation whose result was disastrous was the Munich Agreement. Returning from his negotiations with Adolf Hitler, Chamberlain waved the piece of paper on which the agreement was written, and proudly spoke of 'peace in our time'. He was certain that he had averted the threat that Hitler constituted.

Hitler's perception of the negotiations was completely differ-ent. He saw Chamberlain as compliant and toothless. Hitler thought that Great Britain wouldn't dare intervene if he pursued his expansionary policy. With the agreement secured, Hitler thought he could get away with letting his military machine crush Europe, leaving her in ruins.

One of the few perceptive politicians was Winston Churchill. His comment on the agreement was, 'You had the choice between war and shame. You chose shame, and you will reap war'. Churchill attempted to acquaint himself with Hitler's way of thinking and acting.

One thing he did to do so was to read *Mein Kampf*, in which Hitler had written:

> "History teaches us that states having once given in to an armed threat without being forced to do so, will later accept the most disgraceful humiliations and losses rather than taking up arms. He who has gained such an advantage is well advised to put forward his new demands ... "

Let me shed some light on the various perspectives in a negotiation. You're about to build a garage. You know what the garage should look like, you want good quality, it should be ready by winter, and you don't want to pay more than necessary. You ask three builders to give you an estimate. One of the estimates is somewhat lower than the other two, and consequently you're inclined to let him do the job.

You discover that he is keen to get it. He calls you several times to hear how his bid is compared to the others, and whether you have made up your mind. You see a chance to squeeze the price a bit.

On a Friday afternoon you meet. It's a time that doesn't suit the builder very well. He has very little time, and he tells you that he's already late. At his house out in the country he has invited people to a party. He asks you to be given until Monday to see if he can do anything about the price. You pressurize him by introducing a threat. 'It's hard for me to wait till Monday. I promised Mr. Smith, the builder, that I'd let him know today, and his price is $6000 lower than yours. In that case, I'll probably have to let him have the job.'

These words are followed by an oppressive silence. It's an efficient tactic to squeeze the builder. After a few seconds he says 'OK,

I'll go down by $7000, but then I want the contract now.' He gets the job, and you part. You are proud of having been so clever in having squeezed the lowest bid down by another seven thousand. Money for old rope!

Let's look at this from the builder's perspective. While going home in his motor, the pressure and stress he felt during the negotiation evaporate. He sees the chain of events in a different light. He is annoyed with himself for having been so eager that he let himself be squeezed. He realizes that he won't be able to build the garage at the price you've agreed. He regrets having been in so much of a hurry. He suspects that you might have lied about Mr Smith's quotation. He feels cheated.

He starts thinking about how he can get out of the deal. He recalls that you had reached an agreement about the time the construction work was to begin, but nothing was said about when it was going to be completed. Your garage will just have to be the job he does when he's got nothing else to do. He reviews the possibilities of using cheaper materials, and thinks about how to cut corners without being caught.

He knows that it isn't right to work in this way, it's against his professional pride, but his wish for revenge and his need to get through the financial problems without suffering an undue loss win the day.

In any case, your garage is completed, but not before winter as you had imagined — the quality and finish are less than perfect. You contact legal and construction experts to get their support.

Both experts agree that you've received a shoddy garage, but they advise you not to take the matter to court. It would cost you a lot of time and money, and you'd have to invest a lot of emotions and energy. Your chances of winning aren't all that great, and if you do win, it would only be a pyrrhic victory. You would win on paper, but you wouldn't get enough money to cover your costs. And your garage would still look the same.

The negotiation gain you thought you had made as a buyer when you succeeded in bargaining down the price by $7,000 didn't last long. The cause is that you viewed the negotiation only from your own perspective. Hopefully you've learned your lesson: being right is not the same as winning. A formal, legally binding contract is an important, but not a sufficient condition for things to work out. You must have an opposite number who can and will perform what's been agreed.

Negotiation is a game between two parties and must be viewed from the point of view of both parties in order for you to achieve a good result. The other party must always have sufficient resources to be able to carry out his end of the bargain. If his calculations don't make sense, there's considerable risk that you will both end up worse off.

What are the best negotiation methods?

Many people are looking for a single negotiation approach that will ensure that they always get what they want. Forget it — any such approach doesn't exist. Nor is there any one negotiation method that is always better than all the others. You should combine co-operation and zero-sum games. However, the way in which these two factors are combined will vary from case to case.

Negotiation technique is a science in which you have to work with probabilities, but you must still expect the improbable to happen. You can't predict with complete certainty how the other party is going to perceive of the negotiation you're about to embark on. You can't with complete certainty establish that he perceives your signals as you intended him to do.

> Negotiation technique is a science in which you have to work with probabilities, but you must still expect the improbable to happen.

You can't be sure how he's going to react to your signals, nor which signals he's going to react to. You're uncertain of his needs. You don't know the subconscious needs and feelings governing him. You can't plan your entire negotiation in advance, nor structure it around any definite patent method.

Summary: Choice of strategy

The strategy will be influenced by your own personality and that of the other party, your personal chemistry, your view of the upcoming negotiation, and of the future.

Other issues to consider include the following:

- The policy of the organization, its ethical standards, corporate and industrial culture, and the relative strength of the parties will affect any choice of method.
- Subconscious needs govern the choice of strategy.
- Other cultures are better geared to combat than ours.
- Any negotiation will often consist of both subconscious and unstructured mixes of different strategies.
- Give priority to openness, trust, and co-operation. Keep your fighting spirit and aggressiveness in check.
- Learn to view the negotiation from the point of view of the other party.

7
Not everything can be measured and weighed

Negotiations are far more than processes where everything revolves around the added value and the distribution of the cake. You will experience meetings where you suddenly do not understand the opponent. As far as you are concerned, he has stopped functioning rationally. Value judgements which you have difficulty understanding and accepting seem to be more important than money and measurable facts.

Not everything can be measured in monetary terms or as technical performance. Our decisions cannot be illustrated or explained exclusively by means of fact-finding calculations of an economic or technical nature. There is a further dimension which cannot be measured and which often can be difficult to understand for the people we negotiate with. Perhaps even for us. We have to learn to see more dimensions in a negotiation situation and thus understand the irrational.

On the same street are two hotels some hundred metres apart. They both offer all the types of service which the businessman may need. Both hotels prioritize comfort and safety. The price for a room differs by more than $100. Both hotels have a high occupancy rate. Many of the people who have chosen the expensive hotel could not imagine choosing the cheaper alternative. Why? There are many different answers:

- There is not the same atmosphere.
- Its profile does not fit our image. We do not want anyone to associate us with a low-price alternative.

- Some years ago I stayed at one of their motels and since then I have always associated them with poor service and lousy food.
- The more expensive alternative is part of a well known hotel chain which invests a lot in its trade mark. This is where the rich and the beautiful stay. This is where I want to stay.

In a company where new rules have been introduced directing everybody to stay at the low-price hotel, many people will object. This is difficult for the rational finance manager to understand. He does not share the others' value norms. It is difficult to measure and objectively assess atmosphere and image, which further aggravates the situation. While one person believes that the expensive hotels send out a signal that the company is not cost-conscious, the other argues that the damaging effects of not cherishing its profile will be unheard of.

One person's assessments need not necessarily be more or less right than another person's. But he who does not understand the importance attached to the keywords listed below will have trouble understanding, meeting and earning his opponent's respect.

- Status, profile and class.
- Design.
- Credibility.
- Trade mark.
- Experience.
- Safety.
- Closeness.
- Language and cultural community.
- Atmosphere.
- Political value norms.
- Ethics.
- Fairness.

These keywords can arouse strong feelings which make co-operating difficult or impossible. During the merger attempts between Telia and Telenor, suggestions were made that the contemplated group chief executive, the Norwegian Tormod Hermansen, perhaps did not have the right profile to lead the group out into the world market. This was enough for the entire merger to be questioned immediately.

The attempts to merge Telia and Telenor are surrounded by complexities which are, for many, difficult to measure and understand. The politicians involved were not sensible enough to consider the business aspects of the merger. Individual nations' special interests and prestige were given too much emphasis. All this was embraced by the mass media and blown out of proportion. We all witnessed how all this contributed to preventing the realization of the deal. Money is not important when the negotiations come to be about more important things.

Fairness

Is fairness a just argument for rejecting an otherwise good proposition? Many argue in favour of fair solutions and a fair distribution. Should a member of a local council say no to a company which can contribute a solution to the unemployment problem in his municipality because it is unfair that the company owner should become a millionaire within a short while? To some people it is not fair that others make a lot of money. If these people had the power, would it then be more fair to allow them to make a decision which entails that others cannot get a job?

> Is fairness a just argument for rejecting an otherwise good proposition? Many argue in favour of fair solutions and a fair distribution.

What is fair? And how can it be measured? Is it fair that those in power determine how other people may spend their money? Left-wing politicians who want to prohibit and complicate all private initiative within the school, health and welfare areas always justify this with fairness. It is not fair that he who chooses to spend his money on health services can skip the waiting list. It should not be possible to make money from people who want an alternative education or an alternative employer than state or municipality. On the other hand it is quite fair to buy a Mercedes while others cannot even afford a bicycle. Negotiating with a person who will not abandon his political value judgements can be a completely hopeless task. You will meet no sympathy for solutions where the cake to be shared can be made bigger and benefit all.

Imaginary forms of added value

Skilled marketing people who would like to sell their products, services and ideas try to tempt us with promises of added value. They claim that there is a great added value to be gained from their products, services and trade marks. Added value which they often cannot make visible and concrete for us in an understandable and measurable manner. An added value which apparently can only be found on the psychological level. They have created strong trade marks by means of massive and skilfully devised advertising messages. Trade marks which we identify with. Trade marks which stand for style, class, success image, group identity, status, ethics, awareness of the environment, quality, value for money or mystery. Everything can sell.

Is this 'The Emperor's New Clothes' all over again, or are we talking about real types of added value? That is for you to decide.

When one of us had to invest in two expensive beds, he asked the shopkeeper how big a discount he was willing to give him if he bought the beds from his store and not from one of the ten or so other stockists in Stockholm. Worried, he answered: 'The trade mark [of the bed manufacturers] has such a great incorporated added value that we must not destroy it by giving discounts. We are more or less prohibited from price competition. We shopkeepers keep an eye on each other'.

How true his cartel claim is cannot be entirely assessed but is it obvious that the bed manufacturer has skilfully succeeded in building a strong trade mark, which means that they can demand high prices. There is a clear added value in the sales and production links which can get a significantly higher price because their products are well-known and enjoy a high status. The millions which they invest in advertising come back with interest because of a high price. As a buyer you do not experience any noticeable product advantages of this particular bed compared to other quality makes. The seller did not really succeed in explaining what sort of added value it is you get from buying this type of bed. For us there is no added value in contributing to pay for the advertising which the producer has used to build up his trade mark while there is an obvious status for others in owning a certain make. Depending on our view of the world, we can have an entirely different perception of what constitutes added value.

When one of us had to buy a car, he was offered the comfort, the design as well as the safety package plus the millennium package with many types of added value. When asked where the added value was, the seller answered: 'Compared to our general price list, you make $5,400 if you choose all the packages'. That seems like a mirage to us. The prices in the general price list have been fixed so as to give the buyer the impression that he is getting a good deal and a fantastic discount if he buys extra in the shape of different packages. What is part of the comfort package? Air-conditioning, external thermometer, a drinks holder and a leather wheel. The leather wheel he would never buy no matter how low the price was. Now that is delivered as an accessory so that the seller can use it as an argument for the great added value.

An investment counsellor in a bank tries to convince us of the added value which can be gained by letting him handle and administer our capital. That sounds interesting so we ask him what added value he can offer. He starts to list the different services which the bank can offer; we would have access to the entire bank's expert knowledge; we would be VIP customers and get the bank's newsletter every month for free. As far as we can see, the bank employee offers exactly the same services as all other investment counsellors. Since we do not understand what is so unique about his

> If we do not make visible, in a tangible way, the added value which we offer our partners, our beautiful words will amount to nothing because our reasoning is not credible.

offer, we ask him to explain it more clearly. 'What is it more concretely you offer? Can you guarantee that you are above the index or can you prove that you historically have been some of the best investors of capital in this country?' We are interested and prepared to listen. The bank employee is very shocked that we have dared question the great and, according to him, obvious values which this bank's name offers.

If we do not make visible, in a tangible way, the added value which we offer our partners, our beautiful words will amount to nothing because our reasoning is not credible.

8
What are the prerequisites for a successful co-operation agreement?

The experiences we have told you about so far in this book speak for themselves. Co-operating is not easy and it is often made impossible because the wrong people are assigned to the project. There are a number of basic prerequisites which must be fulfilled if the parties are to have the chance of success.

> Co-operating is not easy and it is often made impossible because the wrong people are assigned to the project.

1. **The human chemistry must be in order.** If there is no human chemistry characterized by mutual respect, trust and openness, the co-operation agreement is doomed to fail. It is people who do business with each other, not computers, and it is people who are assigned to find the optimal prerequisites of the project. Human beings have feelings.

2. **Openness, humility and respect are not always sufficient ingredients.** Enthusiasm and a positive basic view can be equally important. We have met people at the negotiation table who completely lack personal magnetism, which may be needed. All attempts to communicate with them fail. They are silent; there is no repartee. We do perceive the words they are saying but in spite of that we do not understand what they want to tell us. All the signals we are used to, such as eye contact, gesture, intonation, are absent. These people can function very well indeed when they communicate with computers and other machines but when it comes to

associating with other people, they have a problem. Lack of sympathy, understanding and respect for the existing cultural differences can also destroy meetings between people.

3. **Both parties have to believe in the co-operation model.** Being motivated and sacrificing the time it takes, running the risks which are always present, pushing certain of their own value norms aside and adjusting to the surroundings require that the parties have bought the advantages of co-operation. They are totally familiar with the theories. They have realized that the co-operation model is not for 'soft men' and that it can make equally as tough demands as the traditional fighting model. They do not need to be 'macho'.

Rational and knowledgeable negotiators

The knowledge of the things we negotiate about is greatly lacking. In today's slim organizations, bigger and bigger demands are made on the employees. People who have never negotiated before end up in jobs where negotiating is one of their most important duties. We may meet a technician who is expected to be able to handle the business side of negotiations. His lack of business experience and knowledge of economy makes it impossible for him to see the 'deal'. He sees the technical requirement specifications as a challenge. The costs, the time and the risks which the demands result in become vague and a general view of the business is missing. His decisions will not be businesslike.

Knowledge of how different people function and think is missing. Life experience is not sufficient for the necessary humility to be present. The rationale can become unattainable if prestige and personal value norms become too important.

The companies' bookkeeping must take into consideration the total effect of an agreement. It must not be possible for a negotiator to conceal or transfer costs to a 'wrong' account.

Communication skills

Heavy demands are made on communicative competence. Personal magnetism, enthusiasm, the ability to persuade others, being able to sell ones ideas, listening to others and understanding them. We see many negotiators here who fail just before the finishing line. Their attributes may well be first class but they do not succeed in getting their message across. They talk at cross-purposes and there is no offer of a new chance. One of the big problems we have experienced is the lack of good communicators.

Generosity

Many people find it difficult to be generous. Their envy is too strong. Your own assessment of what makes a fair compensation is non-negotiable. If you try to eliminate the opponent's possibilities of achieving a profit, you are in reality cutting off your nose to spite your face.

Creativity

The added value can only arise if we change what is given. The necessary creative forces are up against:

- the conservative person who opposes any change;
- the person who settles and thinks that everything is fine the way it is;
- the person who perceives change as a threat.

Managerial task

It is the management's job to make sure that the right people are assigned to negotiations and projects. Knowledge and skills can be developed. Organizational problems, distribution of responsibility, reward systems and bookkeeping problems which make a general view impossible can be eliminated.

9
Co-operation risks

Co-operation and partnership is no patent medicine which always guarantees a better negotiation result than the traditional zero-sum game. There are different risks which you must be aware of. Is your partner really your partner or is he a fight negotiator trying to take advantage of your openness?

What are the risks?

You have misjudged the opponent's intentions

The catastrophic negotiation in Munich in 1938 is a terrifying example of what can happen if we misjudge the opponent's intentions. After having returned home from negotiations with Hitler, Chamberlain waived an agreement around and talked about peace in our time. He was absolutely convinced that he had averted the threat which Hitler posed. Hitler's experience of the negotiations was an entirely different. He saw Chamberlain as weak, accommodating and spineless. Hitler assessed that Britain would not dare interfere if he continued his expansion. With the agreement in his hand, Hitler dared to let his military engine roll forward and turn Europe into ruins. Churchill was the only politician who was perspicacious and critical of the agreement.

There are plenty of people in the business world and in politics who lack normal inhibitions when it comes to ethics. They display psychotic characteristics. In the beginning they can be courteous, charming and pull the wool over your eyes. They never intend to keep their promises, they are only made in order to make you accept the conditions they have set up.

In exchange for promises of being part of big businesses, many people fall into the trap and invest time, money and expertise in order to help the opponent solve some problems and develop a new technique. They are naive and settle for the opponent's word of future gains. When the opponent then has got what he wants, he does not even say thanks for the effort, he breaks the agreement.

We have encountered large companies which have given away for free and invested many millions in development costs, an investment which their opponent has made them pay by promising to make future series orders at low-price suppliers or by taking the manufacturing in his own hands.

We have also closely studied the buyers who treat their partners this way. The buyers are taught by management to place the development with those who have the necessary knowledge but without any view to future business deals. They prefer to get the supplier to do the work on a purely speculative basis. It is considered smart to make promises which lack any foundation and promises which they know they will never fulfil.

> You will find large well-known companies both among the villains and among those who have been duped. That a person is a known businessperson is no guarantee of high morality.

You will find large well-known companies both among the villains and among those who have been duped. That a person is a known businessperson is no guarantee of high morality.

The narcissistic negotiator

The narcissistic negotiator is a very charming person who makes all his projects seem bigger than they really are. He will do anything to get you involved in the project; you are met with kindness and great interest. You feel flattered by all the courtesy and you will of course do something in return for all the attention you get. It becomes natural to give from your own knowledge, your own contacts and ideas. Then some day everything goes quiet. The opponent does not need you anymore. From being someone praised to the skies, you are now a person he does not want anything to do with. White turns to black.

Agreements are not made to be kept

A legally binding agreement is a good thing but in itself it does not constitute a guarantee that the opponent in fact will keep his part of it. The agreement has been entered into with the purpose of coaxing you into the project and making you do the things you have promised. Consider the following example.

A sub-contractor and a construction company have entered into a partnership in connection with a construction project and have divided responsibility, work and money between them. According to the agreement the contractor shall have the rest of his money, $1 million, when the entire work is complete and an expert's opinion has been consulted. After the expert has given his opinion, he forwards his invoice for the last million. The money does not come and the reminders yield no result. The contractor experiences liquidity problems because he has to pay both salaries and taxes within a week. He calls his partner and asks what has become of the money. He is told that if he wants money, he must send a new invoice, for $800,000 or there will be no money.

The partner is trying to re-negotiate the conditions. He has got the contractor to finish the work, he has got everything he wanted but the contractor is still waiting for some of his money. An unequal balance of power.

The contractor gets furious, he calls the top management, the builder himself and threatens them with both recovery and going to the mass media to warn others against entering into a co-operation agreement with the construction company. The builder is sorry for what has happened and promises to straighten the whole thing out. He will meet the contractor face to face to apologize and hand him a cheque for $1 million. The contractor breathes a sigh of relief; the threat worked.

He meets the builder who apologizes and then hands him a cheque. When the contractor wants to take the cheque, a very tense situation arises because the builder will not let go of it. After a couple of seconds of silence the builder says: 'What would you prefer? The cheque for one million or my assurance that you will be included in more projects?' The contractor, who was totally unprepared for this question, lets go of the cheque. The builder tears the cheque apart and continues: 'So you understand that one million is a bit too much. The project has not gone as well as we expected so it is only fair that you bear some of the costs. $800,000 may be a bit low. I have had a cheque for $850,000 written out to you'. He gives him the cheque, the two men shake hands, the contractor has to sign a paper stating that they have settled the matter amicably.

The agreement turned out to be worthless when the construction company no longer wanted to honour it. It is possible for the contractor to pursue the matter legally in order to force the opponent to pay but will he be able to handle the mental stress, will he be able to handle being excluded from participating in future projects, has he got enough money to be able to wait for the construction company to pay? He is probably not prepared to pay the price needed to win his legal dispute.

How to avoid being duped

In order not to be cheated despite a legally binding agreement we can be forced to make sure that we get our share of the cake. Within the banking system there are different methods to ensure payment and to ensure that the question of payment is not decided by the opponent but by an impartial body.

When our feelings react and our common sense recedes into the background.

> Negotiations are mainly about feelings. If an agreement is made, its content depends to a large extent on how the parties function socially. If they get along well and feel togetherness and respect, it becomes easier to reach an agreement.

Feelings catch on as quick as lightning. Negative and positive signals throw the opponent into a negative or positive mood respectively in a matter of seconds. Long before our consciousness has picked up the signal, we react on it. In other words, we are influenced no matter whether we want to be or not. Negotiators can get carried away and be manipulated when there is chemistry in the room. They stop making rational decisions. In the hands of a unscrupulous person, you can become rather naive.

Fermenta and Volvo: 1986

We find an example of this in the agreement between Fermenta and Volvo in January 1986. The deal was reached extremely quickly which surprised the outside world. But Volvo's CEO P.G. Gyllenhammar explained it this way: 'It has to be quick when you feel there is merging of thoughts and ideas'. The Fermenta agreement ended up costing Volvo $250 million. The day after the agreement had been entered into, it became apparent that Fermenta was a bluff; a house of cards which collapsed when the truth came out.

In his book *Även med känsla*, Bonniers 1991, Gyllenhammar comments on the Fermenta agreement. He starts the chapter on Fermenta with the following words:

> "My wife has told me many times. You must be both naive and have made thousands of mistakes... That is probably true. Naive — perhaps. Impulsive certainly. I am easily turned on when I meet an exciting idea... The Fermenta case... did not come as quickly and surprisingly for me as many have described it... We were prepared for and open towards structural changes in the trade when Refaat El-Sayed appeared in the arena. About his work on the other hand we did not know much more than what had been written and said publicly. But Handelsbanken filled in the blanks on that point... We became one of many victims of their effort even though you can apply your own judgement... I met Refaat El-Sayed for the first time in the new year of 1986... I was captured by the plan... In this new structure Volvo should be a grand owner who dominated in the long run. I liked the idea. We met once more shortly after... The proposal was simple and clear... We were provoked into quickly confirming that an outline existed... The ink was not even dry on our agreement in principle before the first cracks started to appear... The next day it was revealed that he had been lying... Then you check everything another way and differently".

Replacement of people

> Because co-operation is based on human contact and mutual understanding which bind people together in a project, a risky situation arises if the key people are replaced.

The new person has no sense of the spirit of the agreement. It has never been written down. He has not participated in the discussions and considerations which the conditions in the agreement are based on. He may have an entirely different view on what is right and reasonable. His assessments are based on other experiences. His loyalty is somewhere else and he does not feel bound by the things the other have agreed on. He wants to show who he is, mark his preserves and prioritize his own goals and needs.

Attempts at a constructive dialogue are met with the words: 'My predecessor had his own ideas. I work my way and I have been given the job of taking over and finishing the project. I cannot answer for the verbal agreements which others have entered into'.

You are now faced with the choice between swallowing your pride and accepting the situation or attempting to set him straight or re-negotiate and see if despite everything you can find common ground.

You become dependent on the opponent

You have contracted a commercial marriage. If your company is to function, the opponent has to do a decent job. For example, we enter into a training co-operation with another company. We are responsible for development and the contents of the course and they assume responsibility for marketing and arrangement of the courses.

What happens if they make a mess of the marketing? With a view to saving money they can be tempted to reduce their marketing input. The turnover we expect does not come. Our development costs are not covered. They do not pay their teachers well enough and quality is lacking. The course gets a bad name. It falls back on us. It has an effect on all their courses.

We are mutually dependent on each other and in our own interest we have to carry out the control measures we can, we have to make demands on the opponent, have the demands accepted and obtain guarantees within the agreement.

We agree with the wrong person

Do the people we negotiate with have sufficient authority and power to ensure that the agreement is honoured? Must it be approved by others? Will a new owner or management prioritize in an entirely different way? What will happen if other politicians come into power?

We train the opponent

A foreign businessperson wants to come into the market but is dependent on getting a local partner. When the local partner has done his job and built a functional company, the foreigner says 'thanks a lot' and establishes his own sales office. We have trained him. He takes both our knowledge and our customers but it is up to us to pay the costs.

The personal ties grow too strong

It is only natural that friendship grows between people who co-operate; bonds of friendship which can become so strong and important that we do not want to risk them by re-negotiating old agreements the day the external conditions change and give reason for re-evaluating the agreement.

When choosing a partner you prioritize old friends. When placing attractive orders for services you prefer people you know — competence and skills are not considered the highest priorities.

> When choosing a partner you prioritize old friends. When placing attractive orders for services you prefer people you know — competence and skills are not considered the highest priorities.

Monopoly

Companies that co-operate can become too strong and distort competition. This can be found on the sellers' as well as on the buyers' side. Purchase cartels and wage cartels are equally as harmful.

10
Understanding customers' needs

Case study: FKI Logistex

Crisplant A/S is part of the FKI material handling division called FKI Logistex. In 1999/2000, the total turnover of FKI Logistex was £1,332 million. Crisplant A/S is a project-oriented company producing transport and sorting systems, for baggage handling, parcel handling and distribution centres.

Crisplant develops, produces and installs tailor-made solutions adapted to the customers' need for system solutions which improve capacity, efficiency and profitability. Crisplant is the leading producer on the world market, a position Crisplant improves offensively through the development of advanced sorting and logistics systems.

In 2000, Crisplant A/S achieved an order intake of roughly 1.5 billion Danish Kroner.

Crisplant creates a better business by understanding the needs of the customers

Price and quality is not enough in a world where everybody can carry out or copy basic production competencies.

That is why Crisplant is goal oriented in the area of negotiation technique and the ability to understand the needs and business of the customers. Partnering and openness are often the way to success.

> Price and quality is not enough in a world where everybody can carry out or copy basic production competencies.

The idea of partnering was not new to Crisplant. The company has in its own way used elements from partnering in its work with customers for years. So it was not the idea of enhanced partnering which made the Danish company, which has customers in many parts of the world, co-operate with MarketWatch on negotiation technique. The company wanted to give its employees a strong tool which could make them more skilled in the art of negotiation.

The market for logistics solutions for luggage or packaging sorting has changed significantly over the last couple of years. Whereas the company of mostly engineers previously encountered people with the same technical background as themselves, they are encountering more and more professional buyers today who excel in law and economics.

During the same period, many of Crisplant's former partners and customers have shed their skin and today appear in the same business arena as competitors, to fulfil the professional buyers' wish to be able to negotiate for the full service in one place without having an eye to the product's technical complexity.

As a consequence of this development, many buyers and a great deal of Crisplant's competitors focus on price and not so much on the less hard factors such as the ability to deliver the specific function without delays and the reliability of the plant. These are parameters which are expected to be met and for this reason do not form a considerable part of the negotiations but which often can become crucial for the choice of supplier if you can make the customer acknowledge them.

'We work a lot with assessing and analysing the needs of our customers. Not just on the basis of the specific task but also based on our knowledge of the development, the demands others make, and the safety which the customer should expect — and often is dependent on,' says Erik Laursen, CEO. 'That is why we work intensely with the additional values which Crisplant can add to the product and the finished solution. Our ability to render these values visible in relation to the unconscious needs of the customer will make our prices higher than those of our competitors.'

The work with the unconscious needs often mirrored in the additional values which Crisplant delivers is inspired by the Maslow hierarchy of physiological needs where the basic needs are at the bottom. In Crisplant's world, the basic prerequisites are:

- the ability to deliver;
- price;

- high quality;
- time observance;
- good references.

On top of these are the special needs which Crisplant sees as its hallmark and which justify the extra price which Crisplant expects to be able to get. And this is where the word 'partnership' comes in. Erik Laursen explains: 'Crisplant wants to be a better partner than its competitors. This means that we must be skilled at understanding the customer's business. Then we can contribute to developing a solution which neither he nor we could have seen from the beginning. The additional values are then built on the synergy we create together with the customer and the creativity and innovation which we display. So there is more to it than just delivering a physical product.'

The attitudes and a high level of ambition — and not least the ability to fulfil the expectations were in Erik Laursen's opinion the reason why Crisplant got the job when the UK's ParcelForce had to have a new sorting plant, and why Crisplant was subsequently named supplier of the year.

Credibility and trust

Erik Laursen has no doubt that Crisplant has a good product — and also that it is better than the competitors' in a number of ways. But he also knows that the competitors in a number of areas can be a match for Crisplant and in some cases sell cheaper.

'But that does not worry us much. In only a few cases do we spend time discussing the physical product itself with the customer. On the other hand we spent a lot of time talking about functionality and analyzing the needs of the customer. Today the main element is the flexibility of the software and the possibility of expanding and scaling the plant to the demands of the future.'

'Many of our competitors make good products. That is why it is so important to be able to put yourself in the customer's place and understand his needs and development. This enhances our credibility, and the customer feels safe when he feels that we listen and do not leave him or her in the lurch. Our commitment and our ability to generate ideas for solutions are strong in relation to our customers.'

'We keep our promises. This means that we do not spend our time on the law when problems occur but find a solution. The law can always be dealt with subsequently.'

This attitude — and the ability to prove that it also works in reality — fits according to Erik Laursen well with the cornerstones of partnering: credibility, openness and flexibility.

'For Crisplant its presence in the minds of the customers is significant. The co-operation must develop in a way where we are involved as a natural partner before big investment decisions are made. This increases our chance in the order game.' 'And if we are able to live up to our own demand of being the best in the world within our business area, there is a really good chance that the customer says that he also would like to buy some of our after-sales products. And it may be in this period that we have the possibility of good, stable earning.'

After-sales services and supplementary tasks are crucial to maintain customer relations. While a project for the development of a sorting plant may take up to two years, there will often be an after-sale time horizon with continuous sale to the customer of 10–15 years.

'This means eventually that we slowly but surely work towards a mutual loyalty which is very important both for us and for our customers. In some cases the trust is so big that a hand-written note on our presentation is sufficient for us to go ahead with the task,' Erik Laursen stresses.

He points out that this trust does not mean that Crisplant sets the price but that the customer evaluates the market conditions from time to time and is aware of what similar deliveries cost at the competitors.

Solid homework

Crisplant has no specific product to present in connection with the sales work. Each product is tailor-made to the customer according to the special functions which the customer wants and the physical boundaries for the plant.

'We sell on references from our customers to a very high degree. Often new customers have visited one of our existing customers to hear how it was to work with Crisplant in the project phases.

For this reason we must always be the best in terms of our ability to deliver the agreed quality on time and within the budget agreed with the customer. This makes high demands on our organization and on our employees,' Erik Laursen concludes.

Crisplant works seriously with the building up of the employees' competencies so that everyone involved in a project always knows what the task is and what is expected of each individual in the project group.

> everyone involved in a project always knows what the task is and what is expected of each individual in the project group.

This happens through the project management training which all project employees go through. And Crisplant has included a big part of its experience from this work in the development of a shared knowledge of how the company tackles negotiations with customers and creates the best prerequisites for partnering.

The Human Resource Manager at Crisplant explains that all development initiatives in the department must be business oriented. Therefore the purpose of improving the project managers' negotiation ability is also to make them more skilled at pursuing Crisplant's business strategy: To create relations with the customers and develop the projects in a partnership with the customer.

'The partnership which is formed with the customer can be described as a spiral where we come closer and closer to the customer. We can only do this if we can create value for the customer — and for ourselves through the partnership. That is why we are here,' the Human Resource Manager says.

The value to the customer, of course, lies in the fact that Crisplant has delivered a solution and consultancy beyond what could be expected because we have used our knowledge about the customer's business, market development and the technological development. The value to Crisplant lies according to the Human Resource Manager in the fact that the company has achieved various relationships with the customer through the partnership and hopefully will be able to keep him as a customer for many years to come.

'We do not only view the partnership in light of the negotiation situation but more in the light of the firm relations. We have to be able to create win-win results together with the customer in such a way that we do not forget to win ourselves. We have a business to run,' the Human Resource Manager explains.

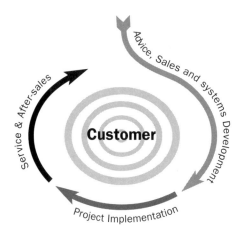

'This means that we have to be skilled negotiators and create a greater revenue for Crisplant in a way where the customer does not feel run over but where he also can see the real extra values which the negotiations have given him.'

'To sit with the customer in the moment of truth is a significant part of the negotiations. Another part is to handle the project so that we are the best in the world within our business area.'

Changed behaviour

For the Human Resource Manager the ability to negotiate and manage projects is a building up of a competence with a long-term goal, since competence building in a number of ways only will succeed when people are ready to change their behaviour.

'The human competence is built on behavioural development and if we build on cross-organizational competence, it will end up as organizational development. Our project training is an expression of what started as a typical project management training and then developed into organizational development,' the Human Resource Manager points out. Three-quarters of Crisplant's 400 white collar employees have gone through project training.

'The project training covers a lot of tools, techniques and methods which together have made us good at finishing projects. The negotiation part is just as important for the expression we leave behind when we leave the customer because it has made us better at handling the situation with the customer here and now.

Today the negotiation competence is a natural part of Crisplant's project training. For this reason the employees at Crisplant have added a number of elements from the project training to the negotiation preparation. This also applies to the term 'anchorman'.

The role of the anchorman is to keep his colleagues on track during the training of the new methods and the preparations for a negotiation and to say stop when the discussion of possibilities and scenarios are moving away from the line which should lead them to the target.

'The training in preparing together with an anchorman is almost more important than the negotiation course. It is in everyday work that the negotiation competence is developed: from consciousness about negotiation techniques to a skill which you naturally draw on in the situation.'

'If we do not focus on the in-house training, we will not get the effect of what the employees have learned. And it is also here that we get the consciousness about negotiation incorporated in the whole company.

MarketWatch Management has, since 2000, been carrying out consultancy and in-house training for projects and senior managers, operating project from $1 million to $25 million in Asia, Europe, South America, the US and Middle East.

Example 1: Plane tickets cleared the way

The sum of £250,000 divided the parties when Crisplant entered the final negotiations about a job for a big British airline company. The British, who at the end phase were represented by ten people versus Crisplant's single representative, had difficulty accepting Crisplant's bid which was significantly in excess of what the British immediately could accept.

The first negotiations went slowly. The project manager had enough on his plate just answering questions. There was no time to think either constructively nor creatively. But when the customer first reduced his negotiation team to six and later two, the negotiations got underway and creativity flowed.

For this reason a total solution was agreed on where the British airline paid two-thirds of the difference which divided the parties and made a number of additional services available. This included

40 plane tickets between Aarhus and London, free rental car for the entire project period, fork-lift trucks for hoisting tasks in connection with the completion of the project and agreed staffing levels.

For Crisplant the experience was that it takes time to find this type of solution and that there must be an equal relation between negotiators.

Example 2: Partnering with sub-contractors

In connection with the establishing of a luggage sorting plant for an international airport in the Middle East, Crisplant needed a sub delivery of 150 belt units, which is a special component to an estimated price of several million Danish Kroner.

The project manager at Crisplant chose three possible contractors which were allowed to bid on the job. He decided to start negotiations with two of them.

Crisplant already knew that contractor (X) would be able to deliver a solution which Crisplant could live with. It would be solid, reliable and affordable. But it would also be fairly elderly, technologically speaking.

The other contractor (Y) had the ability to deliver a product approaching the state of the art and whose sophisticated design with respect to image and profile would fit Crisplant's total solution well. But Crisplant was also aware that the price was too high compared to what could be afforded on the project.

Before the negotiations began, the project manager worked out a script for the course and analyzed the possible variable elements in the two bids. He also decided not to negotiate about the price at first, but just to indicate that it was too high – and that the solution should contain a price adjustment and adjustments in the shape of the delivery.

The meeting with contractor X was relatively short even though the bid was favourable with respect to price if one looked at the price alone. Contractor X got somewhat confused when Crisplant only wanted to talk about requirements and technical design. Crisplant had a long list of specific demands for which they wanted assurance. Contractor X was somewhat reluctant in accepting the requirements and also somewhat reluctant in the negotiation of new solutions and any other possibilities. The negotiation ended with contractor X going home encouraged to present a proposal of how to come closer to an agreement.

Except for a few calls, the dialogue was never followed up and nothing came of it.

Things went differently with contractor Y whose bid was about 20 per cent higher. The representative quickly grasped that Crisplant was very interested in doing business with him but that it was necessary to go through the bid carefully to find areas where the German producer could meet Crisplant's demands. During the negotiations the two parties took several breaks but a result was achieved which both parties could accept.

Crisplant got the desired technical solution at an acceptable price compared to the original bid. On the other hand Crisplant accepted a cheaper solution on sub-covering and agreed to assemble the elements on site which saved contractor Y a significant transportation cost.

Crisplant's experience was that with thorough preparation and openness, co-operation with an adversary that is open and willing to negotiate will make rapid progress.

Additional information about Crisplant or FKI can be found on their websites at www.crisplant.com or www.fkilogistex.com

Crisplant's experience was that with thorough preparation and openness, co-operation with an adversary that is open and willing to negotiate will make rapid progress.

11
The ugly duckling expects a little more ...

Case Study: NCC Corporation–Partnership is a state of mind

The market for building contractors in the Nordic countries is $29.7 billion per year.

NCC Corporation is the biggest group of contractors in Scandinavia with more than 25,000 employees and a total net turnover of $4.75 billion. The market share is around 16 per cent.

NCC is represented in Sweden, Denmark, Norway, Finland, Poland and Germany and has an international division.

Being in an industrial sector with profit margins below 3 per cent makes special demands on flexibility, creativity and development. The desire for and even the possibility of an increased investment in the future has also been limited to less than 1.5 per cent compared to the motor, chemicals and manufacturing industries.

Perhaps this is exactly why the construction sector has been accused of lacking development and forward pointing profiling for many years.

Previously NCC was often told: 'You are too expensive' 'you are not good enough' or 'you are too slow'.

NCC works consciously at placing partnership-based projects with the project managers who can handle the co-operation model.

'Without the commitment of the top management you cannot talk about partnership. The trust which is the basis of real and open co-operation in the shape of partnership can only be created with management commitment,' says Torben Biilmann, CEO of NCC Byg. Over the last couple of years he has been working towards changing the turnover of the construction group so that a greater part of the turnover will come from co-operation agreements.

Competence development

An organization like NCC has been transformed from the traditional craftsman's company into a highly advanced service organization. At the same time there has been a shift of focus and potential towards what is possible and interesting.

In accordance with the traditional methodology a project manager was a 'technician'. 'In a world where competition is intensified, there is far more focus on competence, personal knowledge and credibility,' says Susanne Kynne Frandsen, HR manager.

> 'In a world where competition is intensified, there is far more focus on competence, personal knowledge and credibility,'

Today it is normal, for example, that the project manager is chosen for the person he is just as the client often asks for the person's CV before accepting the project. NCC is very conscious of the human factor and makes use of renowned analytical tools when establishing a project team in order to ensure empathy between the parties. At the same time, the partners' differences and strengths are illustrated and a basic acceptance is created of the differences between people.

All new production employees form part of a three-stage rocket which introduces them to the partnership concept:

- step 1 is a general introduction to partnership;
- step 2 is a seminar directed towards the production;
- step 3 is a continuation of the first seminar directed towards the project manager.

There is furthermore general training in the shape of seminars and evaluations directed towards communicative competence and negotiation technique.

This is to make the employees conscious of the fact that partnership importance and functionality is about more than just improved sales and a chance of increased earnings.

Credibility training

The human factor is the Alpha and Omega of a success-
ful partnership project. 'If trust or personal chemistry is missing, we
will have to replace the participant to promote the project', states
Torben Biilmann.

'Credibility is the basis of partnership', states Torben
Biilmann. That is why Susanne Kynne Frandsen is responsible for carrying out and implementing a number of seminars with the purpose of
creating a consciousness of communication and negotiation competence among the project and planning managers.

One of the measurable results is that the NCC group has
moved more than 50 places up in an annual image study carried out by
a renowned media firm in Scandinavia. 'To us it obviously means
incredibly much that we can land deals worth USD 100 million where
we have been chosen due to our ability to fulfil the clients needs and
wants with respect to quality and not just because of our price,' Torben
Biilmann elaborates.

This is equal to every fourth turnover dollar stemming
from a building project based on partnerships. And if Torben Biilmann
could choose for himself, the partnership model would constitute a far
greater part of the group's building jobs.

'That will, however, require that we become even better at
handling the partnership concept. And it will entail increased employee
training because to a high extent partnership success is based on the
company's ability to make a com-
mitment at a high moral level.'

'Your promises to
partners can only be fulfilled if
the attitudes and the method of
working are deeply rooted in
the organization,' Torben
Biilmann says.

'Your promises to partners can only be fulfilled if the attitudes and the method of working are deeply rooted in the organization.'

Many years' experience

The concept of partnerships is not new to NCC. The group
has, for many years, been working with its own model for co-operation

agreements, and it contains many of the partnership disciplines according to Torben Biilmann.

'We have developed our way of working with partnerships through many different building co-operation agreements. That is why we always start any co-operation by explaining our perception of partnership.'

NCC has a standard model for co-operation and partnership, and it is always adjusted to fit the actual building job.

'We normally always begin with an obligatory kick-off meeting where all the parties on the partnership team relate their success criteria for the job. This is then boiled down to the success criteria of the project. One of these criteria is of course that all participants have a desire to make money for the company, which has to be accepted by all,' says Torben Biilmann.

'If you cannot accept that the other parties run a fair business and wish to make money on their business, you should not enter into a partnership agreement.'

Torben Biilmann emphasizes NCC's rooted culture as one of the reasons why the group is successful in using the partnership model today.

'With a rooted culture you have the framework for creating trust among the employees that the decisions they make are the decisions the rest of us would make, too. And this again creates the necessary trust in NCC Byg with our partners.'

Great potential in the building industry

The advantage to the building trade is obvious. The way things are done today it is almost the rule that additional expenses of up to 15 per cent of the total building costs will arise. This is why there is a lot of money to be made both for the clients and the contractors.

The partnership model for the building industry is based on the idea that the partnership team gets together to prioritize the many million dollars which are available for a building project. This means that the team assesses the project to find the places where

savings can and must be made in order to have money to fulfil special needs. The team also decides how much money to allocate to unforeseen expenses.

That is why the price is fixed from the beginning so to speak, and the client only has to pay extra if he asks for changes on the macro level; for instance a building extension of 2,000 square metres.

All participants on the partnership team play with their cards on the table. Everybody knows what the calculations have been based on. That is why everybody also knows how the money is to be distributed in connection with unforeseen expenses and in case of slight changes to the building project.

'If some parts of the house become more expensive, you have to find savings in the other parts to keep the expenses within the budget'.

'Increased use of partnerships can and must remove the waste for the benefit of all the participants in the building project. For us there is much money to be made from optimizing the building process itself. We have the distribution agreements which form a fixed part of the many partnership agreements'.

In the distribution agreement, the parties have determined, in advance, how a possible profit on the building project is to be distributed, and this is the incentive to work in a more structured manner, to show consideration for the other participants in the project and generally to do things slightly smarter.

'As a rule the distribution scale takes its starting point in the risk factors involved in the building project. It is often 50/50 but it can be different.

There are similarly many models for the distribution of expenses in the event of delay to the building work.

'If, for instance, we have guaranteed that the building project will be kept within the agreed price, then we have to pay the additional expenses. In other cases we may have agreed on a distribution of 1 to 2 with the client', says Torben Biilmann.

Insight into the client's or the subcontractor's situation

Openness and honesty are essential in partnerships. In order to establish these, NCC's customers participate in internal meetings or presentations relating the objectives, demands and expectations

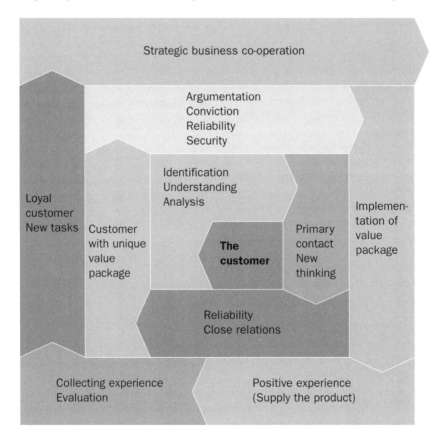

of the organization. 'We are no longer presenting ourselves as sellers,' says Torben Biilmann. 'Instead we start by asking about the customer's wishes and needs. Perhaps we invite them on a trip to Berlin to see the latest in building technology.'

'It is all about us understanding the customer, perhaps even better than he understands himself. We have to be able to identify the job before we can create a value package for the customer and establish the trust which is so essential in any negotiation.'

> 'It is all about us understanding the customer, perhaps even better than he understands himself. We have to be able to identify the job before we can create a value package for the customer and establish the trust which is so essential in any negotiation.'

Savings on fewer disputes

A significant advantage of partnerships is the reduced number of disputes. Previously far too many building cases led to litigation according to Torben Biilmann; this is very costly both for the clients and the contractors and creates an absolute lose-lose situation.

'It is like throwing money out of the window. We will neither get more nor better building work for the money we spend on lawyers' and court fees,' emphazises Torben Biilmann

'By having one board settling disputes, the partnership model saves us that waste of money.'

The board is the top level in the partnership model, and it has been set up to ensure that disputes never go to court. Below the board you will find the control group which closely follows the building work and the project group which is formed to control and carry out the project.

'The fact alone that we have the board is in itself a motivation for settling disagreements and disputes at a far earlier time. That is why we have never experienced that disputes have ended up with the board', Torben Biilmann says.

Public challenge

It is especially in the private building market that NCC building activities have been based on co-operation agreements and the partnership model. Denmark's biggest client, the public, has, however, been locked by EU rules for public tenders.

'It has blocked the municipalities and the counties from using the advantages of the partnership concept. According to a circular they needed drawings made and the building job put out to tender in order to get a low price,' explains Torben Biilmann.

'Public clients have in the last couple of years had a number of bad experiences with building cases where both price and time of delivery had been exceeded significantly. Those experiences along with knowledge from abroad where partnership in the building sector is far more common have given public clients the courage to get started.'

Public clients from Great Britain, Scotland and Australia are particularly far ahead with partnerships. Their experiences show savings between 5–20 per cent. And these ideas have now come to Denmark, where there is a strong development in the public towards partnerships.

However, NCC believes that the group can create added values of up to 30 per cent in many partnerships.

Training

Susanne K. Frandsen and Torben Biilmann emphazise that the basic principles behind partnership are rooted in the organization. They are not just fancy words in the general presentation of the company. That is why most of NCC Byg's project managers have learned about negotiating partnerships over the last couple of years.

'Handling the building work in a partnership agreement makes demands on the employees. They must be capable of listening to and accepting the interests of the partners at the same time as they are fighting for the group. In return it is also very motivating to work together to create something and not having to fight to get the last single invoice in place every day.'

'It requires training, and training is what our project managers get. But since our building jobs are different — every other is won on price alone — the great challenge is to find out whether the same person can handle both types of building projects.'

'Can you fight hard for every dollar one day and then change your behaviour and co-operate the next? We probably have to realize that some employees are best suited for partnership cases whereas others get their small victories by defeating others.'

'On the other hand, our customers are different, too. The customer chooses whether he wants to play whist or bridge, and as a company we are capable of playing both games at a high level.'

Just as it makes great demands on the employees' attitude and training to enter into a partnership agreement, NCC also makes great demands on the clients and other partners who enter into a partnership project. If builders and/or consultants are judged not to be able to live up to the requirements for a partnership agreement, such an agreement will not be entered into.

Consulting engineers

Even though the parties in the building sector have been discussing new ways of co-operating continuously over the last couple of years, it is not until now that the use of the partnership model gathers headway. Conservatism and the fear of losing earnings has been acting as a brake.

'The contractor comes much closer to the client in the case of partnerships. Many are sceptical about this and would prefer that the contractor keeps his place in the building hierarchy. But neither consulting architects nor engineers should have any fear of losing their jobs. In connection with partnerships they will simply be employed by us and not, as previously, by the client. And in many cases it will also be to the great advantage of the consultant to be working for us,' believes NCC.

His explanation is that the EU directorate requires consulting services in excess of \$187,500 to be put out to tender. This means that the consultants, too, are forced to compete on the raw price and not the core competence: professional building consultancy.

'There is always one who is hungry and therefore dumps the price. That is not how we do business. Consultancy is consultancy, and we pay the price which good advice costs. We can not normally accept price competition for consulting services. We only want to look at competencies and quality in that field, and we choose the consultant we want,' states Torben Biilmann.

'For us much, much money is saved by having the right consultant who also can afford to enter the project whole-heartedly and who does not have to sit and dabble in a half percentage. Otherwise it ends up as kids' work for the youngest in the drawing department'.

New challenges

NCC's ambitions for the future are great. The group wants to expand the use of partnerships in order to land the best building jobs and the best employees.

'We are a group which emphazises development both in the group and among the employees. For this reason we have not had much trouble in getting the employees we want. But it has also been of importance that we have worked goal-oriented at changing our reputation since the mid 1990s,' says Torben Biilmann.

From being a contracting company which was more than fit for fight, the style has been changed so that NCC is now seen as a modern, negotiation-oriented building group whose goal of optimizing the building sector is shared by clients as well as consultants.

> NCC is now seen as a modern, negotiation-oriented building group whose goal of optimizing the building sector is shared by clients as well as consultants.

This development will continue in the years to come, with NCC working on expanding the partnership concept to include the largest of the group's regular sub-contractors as well.

'We have to be able to draw on knowledge and experience from our subcontractors and this can only be achieved if we co-operate in accordance with the partnership model,' Torben Biilmann concludes.

NCC has only started using the partnership model on the group's own 6,000 subcontractors today.

'It is quite simply too many partners for us to incorporate the partnership model. When the number of subcontractors has been cut down to a tenth within a short time, we will start working with partnerships with the most suited partners. When the experiences from that work have been clarified, partnerships will become a fixed part of some of our supply agreements,' NCC predicts.

'But it will also make great demands on our subcontractors. They have to have the competence to work with the openness which partnership requires,' emphazises Torben Biilmann, who believes that most of the subcontractors will be competent to handle partnerships in the future.

Partnerships in real life

Over the last couple of years, NCC has been involved in a number of cases using partnerships as basis. Now around 20 per cent of all turnover is based on partnerships, and Torben Biilmann expects a rise to 35 per cent in the near future.

In a number of publicized projects NCC has created real added values of up to $12.5 million in co-operation with the client.

A valuable extra gain is the fact that the employees generally find partnerships more rewarding. They enrich their job function and motivation increases, which results in lower staff turnover.

Torben Biilmann has written *Partnering in Practice* for NCC in co-operation with the parties from the building sector, a guide to partnering which shows ways to establish and carry out the rules of partnerships.

For a number of years MarketWatch Management has held seminars about negotiation technique and the creation of added value for the NCC group.

Further information about NCC can be found on the company's website at www.ncc.se.

12
The value of partnering is based on the strength of the employees

Case study: Hilton Hotel Group and Scandic Hotels — adding value

When Scandic Hotels makes partner agreements with suppliers of, for instance linen and articles for personal hygiene the actual assets are the people involved. The wish and the will of the employees to participate in the development of solutions generates a team spirit and strengthens the position of Scandic Hotels as a strong brand within the Nordic hotel industry.

Scandic is a dedicated hotel operator and leases the majority of its properties at variable rents based on sales. It had 133 hotels in the Nordic markets of Sweden, Denmark, Finland and Norway as of year-end 2000. Outside these countries, Scandic operates 21 hotels.

Scandic's profitability is based on a strong brand, high customer satisfaction, active sales and marketing, and high cost efficiency. Key principles in the business are value for money and care and concern for the guest. Great emphasis is placed on continual competence development for employees at all levels of the organization. Scandic's financial performance is linked to community involvement and environmental sustainability.

Scandic is an organization that is governed by values. Through goal-oriented, continual and long-term effort, the company is promoting common values that forge cohesiveness in the chain and give employees in-depth understanding of the service concept 'Omtanke', which translates to positive, caring , attention, and how it should be expressed in their daily work and in encounters with guests, colleagues, owners and society. This ensures that customers enjoy a consistent, positive experience no matter which Scandic hotel they visit. In the end, the customers' opinion of their stay with Scandic depends on how they are treated by the employees.

To enhance operational efficiency in individual hotels and the chain as a whole, each hotel is run like a 'company within the company.' This is combined with the benchmarking system, Best In Class (BINC). The management concept also includes other systems for marketing and service development, etc.

In Scandic Hotels, partnership is colloquially referred to as *'exploiting synergies.'* This term has been developed in the hotel chain over many years and the meaning of it is deeply rooted in the organization of Scandic Hotels and in the individual hotels.

'We work with partnering or *exploiting synergies* in many fields. Both externally in relation to our service partners and internally in relation to our employees. In both fields it is natural to locate the areas in which we can create added value together. Thus, the phenomenon exploiting synergies has also been brought into the loyalty programmes — also known as the Scandic Club — of the hotel chain, ' says Hans Axel Kristensen, Senior Vice President, Corporate Director Human Resources Management and Competence Development.

'Today all our hotels must work in close collaboration with their suppliers and the local business sector in making offers to the regular customers. The hotel manager is given the opportunity to present his hotel and his restaurant in a form which is not only about his product, but which also gives our guests an opportunity to taste different wines and receive favourable offers or to see and hear a presentation of new car models from, for instance, Audi,' says Hans Axel Kristensen.

This kind of presentation — also known as 'Scandic Club Evenings/Arrangements' — and customer maintenance is of great value for both parties. The hotel maintains and cares for its loyal customers (the Scandic club members) giving them positive experiences while the wine supplier and the car dealer build relations with new prospective customers.

'But otherwise the partnering or constructive co-operation is primarily used in our supplier relations. Scandic Hotels is a hotel chain with a brand identity. Popularly speaking this means that the facilities and the offers found in a Scandic Hotel in Helsinki should be equivalent to those found in a Scandic Hotel in Copenhagen, Stockholm or Oslo.'

'For that reason it is essential that we maintain a close and developing co-operation with our suppliers. They must be motivated to listen to our needs and they must be capable of meeting them.'

The suppliers become partners

When Scandic Hotels goes on the offensive to market itself as a hotel chain — not to be confused with a chain of hotels — with a big social commitment and a wish to be accountable, the suppliers are involved, whether they like it or not.

'We outsource as many tasks as possible. For that reason we do not always have the key to the solution of a problem ourselves and thus we must convince our suppliers that it is a good idea,' says the manager of environment and security issues of Scandic Hotels.

This department has been involved in a large number of development projects in the hotel chain because it is often the question of solving environmental issues or security problems which brings the Scandic Hotels and the partners together.

'In the environmental area we wish to have the lead. This means a lot when we ask a supplier to find a more environmentally desirable solution. For instance we told our regular laundry that we would no longer accept the use of optical brightener and chlorine. They found a solution which we could approve.'

The laundering of all linen, towels, mats and uniforms for Scandic Hotels is carried out by Berendsen Textile. The co-operation in finding new ways of doing things also includes logistics and solutions in benefit of the working environment.

In addition to a clearly defined co-operation concerning solutions and service the hotel chain is also frequently involved in a co-operation with suppliers concerning the training of Scandic Hotels employees. This is exemplified by the co-operation with Henckel EcoLab and different salvage corps.

'Today we use a cleaning system developed in co-operation with Henckel. From the very beginning we have profited by the results and we don't even contribute to the covering of the development costs. During the process we found out that the final result of the development work would be optimal if Henckel also undertook the training of the maids in order for them to make the most efficient use of the cleaning materials.'

The co-operation with safety and security suppliers began with a wish to save money. This became the beginning of a dialogue about the need for security training, fire drills, and maintenance of safety equipment in the hotels.

Partnering is created by human will

The employees are an essential resource in the co-operation with the suppliers. This is primarily due to the fact that a hotel is nothing in itself. It is the employees — the human resource.

'We continuously make every effort to create beautiful and interesting surroundings in our hotels the bricks, the furniture and the interior only constitute a frame. The atmosphere of the hotel – the one that we experience and remember — is created by the employees. And this is also true when it comes to our current co-operation with our regular suppliers concerning the development and the refinement of the products that we buy.'

'The employees are a major part of our co-operation concepts. They are the ones who test and comment on new solutions before we implement them. For that reason their commitment and their wish to participate in change processes are essential. In return both Scandic Hotels and the supplier benefit greatly from the involvement of the employees'.

In the initial phase the supplier receives comments and knowledge from those employees who will actually be working with the product. Later on the input from the employees is about their experiences working with and testing the product in the work process day after day. This knowledge can be turned into improvements and the supplier can thus develop a product with far more market potential than otherwise.

For Scandic Hotels it is a value in itself that the employees engage in the process of exploiting synergies with the supplier and draw on their knowledge and experience. But the hotel chain also has the value of a more motivated and committed staff. Among other things this means that Scandic Hotels today can trace a tendency of greater stability among the staff members with lower turnover. This tendency is expressed through a more profitable operation and less expenses in connection with the hiring and training of new employees.

'For that reason those employees who are actively involved in for instance testing and development receive immediate and thorough feedback from us and from our suppliers. They should know that their contribution to the development work is valuable in order for them to be willing to participate the next time as well.'

Many of the development projects in which the hotel chain participates also have a direct influence on the employees' working day. First, the many projects have brought about a positive financial development for Scandic Hotels and, second, the result has often been an improvement of the working environment. The latter is for instance evident in the co-operation with Henckel EcoLab where the objective was to remove dangerous chemicals from the cleaning products, and with Berendsen Textile where the co-operation has reduced the number of heavy lifts considerably.

Example 1: ETAGE

Every day the maids at the Scandic Hotels change the linen on a great number of beds and send at least the same number of towels to the laundry. This not only represents a big cost on the hotel budgets it also used to mean a lot of heavy lifting and the transportation of a large amount of linen.

Today the hotels use the linen and service system, ETAGE, which is developed by Swedish Tvättmann, a subsidiary company under Berendsen Textile. ETAGE is a small cart packed with the exact number of towels, sheets, and duvet covers needed by the maid. This reduces excessive use and improves the logistics.

Scandic Hotels has, in collaboration with Berendsen Textile, further developed ETAGE in order to meet the need for waste sorting and the demand that the maids have room for cleaning materials, replacement brochures, etc.

Example 2: Formulator

Henckel EcoLab of Germany has, together with Scandic Hotels, developed the cleaning system, Formulator. Today this system is used in every hotel in the chain and Henckel EcoLab has had great success selling the system to many other clients.

The project was initiated by a strongly environmental thinking. Scandic Hotels wished to reduce the use of health hazardous and environmentally damaging cleaning materials without reducing the quality of the hygiene.

The solution was Formulator where all the cleaning materials are mixed immediately before the use. In each hotel there are four 25 litre tanks containing the raw material for the cleaning products. By means of a computer the fluids are mixed and tap water is added.

The result is a noticeable reduction in the use of chemicals, less allergy incidents, an accurate dosage, and consequently less waste.

Today Henckel EcoLab also provides training for Scandic Hotels.

The two above-mentioned examples have among other things contributed to the fact that Scandic Hotels over a four-year period has been able to reduce its energy consumption per guest by more than 13kWh per day. Water consumption has been reduced by more than 30 litres per night and unsorted waste has been reduced by 400 grams per guest per night.

The successful 'Resource hunt', a corporate program promoting the efficient use of resources that was carried out in Nordic hotels between 1997–1999, helped reduce carbon dioxide emissions by more than 15 per cent and to reduce energy costs by more than 20 per cent. This program is now being implemented on an international scale.

Example 3: Security

'You are Scandic's best security officer' is the fundamental thesis of every aspect of Scandic´s Security Program.

For many years Scandic Hotels has co-operated with different salvage corps, in the fields of security and training of security personnel.

This co-operation was initiated when the hotel chain, in search of savings, wanted a joint subscription to the services of safety and security instead of having the hotels subscribe individually. This was the beginning of a dialogue about the need for security, conveyance of patients, and training in the Scandic Hotels.

Today Scandic Hotels and suppliers have an agreement on co-operation which ensures that the security conditions and the security training of the hotels always meet the legal requirements. Furthermore, all employees carry out fire and evacuation drills once a year with the supplier as instructor and sparring partner. The instruction and the drills take place in the hotels so that the employees do not have to adapt the knowledge and the training from a school to the hotel world, but have received the theoretical and practical instruction in their usual working environment.

The agreement with the suppliers also includes the access to assistance from the corps of emergency psychologists employed by the suppliers.

Scandic Hotels is a hotel chain determinedly working on becoming the strongest brand within the hotel industry. The chain wishes to obtain this position by developing and extending its role as an attractive place of work, enriching people, the society, and other interested parties, and becoming an important factor in the local communities where the chain is represented.

At the beginning of 2001 Scandic Hotels owned 153 hotels in Sweden, Finland, Norway, and Denmark while the chain operated an additional 21 hotels outside the Nordic countries. In total Scandic Hotels is represented in 10 countries. In 1999 the 6,600 employees of Scandic Hotels brought in an annual turnover of $75 billion. This yielded a profit of 354 million Swedish Kroner or 6.7 per cent of the annual turnover.

Scandic Hotels is quoted on the Stock exchange in Stockholm, Sweden.

At the time of writing, Hilton Group plc had made a public offer for Scandic, the value of which corresponds a price of $955 million. Scandic's board of directors unanimously recommended that its shareholders accepted the offer. Payment is to be made partly in cash and partly in shares

With this purchase the Hilton Group almost doubles its number of hotels on the European continent and especially in

Scandinavia since 55 hotels will be added to the 65 which Hilton already own.

It is expected that the synergy effect will make it possible to save DKK 200 million in costs from the year 2003, among other things because of the transition to a joint reservation system. In the future the Scandic Hotels will be named Hilton. Hilton which is one of the world's best known trade marks has offered premium to the shareholders of Scandic Hotels AB in order to effectively enter the Scandinavian market with a foundation of more than 153 hotels. The board of Scandic Hotels AB has approved and recommended the sale to the international group of shareholders.

'Scandic shall maximize value growth for shareholders and everything we do must, in the long term, contribute to profitability. That also applies to *Scandic in Society*. It takes a long time to build a good reputation, but it can be destroyed in 15 minutes.

Scandic in Society is an approach that is ultimately manifested in the actions of every employee and which is based firmly on our mission. To maintain and enhance good relationships with our customers and our business environment, while also becoming the most sought-after employer in our industry, it is critical that we assume our responsibility as a good corporate citizen. In this way, we can create a basis of shared values and strengthen our brand and finances and all the while contribute to the society in which we do business.' (Roland Nilsson, CEO.)

13
Knowledge of one's own qualities and costs improves the chance of successful partnering

Case study: TV2 Advertising

TV 2 Advertising is happy to put advertising spots on the air. But not at any cost. Partnering begins with professional consultancy. And it may be a polite 'no thanks' to income if advertising spots in prime time give the advertiser more heartache than joy. That sort of advice is, on the other hand, almost always a guarantee for future co-operation.

TV 2 Advertising's priorities have changed significantly over the last couple of years. Despite the fact that TV 2 provides the only possibility for reaching all Danish households with a TV spot, the partly licence-financed TV station is no longer the absolute first choice when the big advertisers have millions for TV advertising at their disposal. Today TV 2 increasingly has to accept its role as supplement to the Kinnevik-owned TV 3 and the American-dominated TV Danmark's network of local stations.

The new division of roles has also affected the working methods and the self-knowledge at TV 2 Advertising which, independently of TV 2, is responsible for the sale of the costly advertising minutes. While TV 2 Advertising in the first couple of years of its life saw itself as a sparring partner for the advertisers and their consultants (advertising and media agencies), today there is general awareness that, to a far greater extent than before, it is a selling organization with professional expertise within consultancy on the use of TV advertising.

The transformation has challenged both salespeople and management at TV 2 Advertising and made great demands on a changed awareness of sparring and consultancy, cost price and not least sale and additional sale. One of the tools in the transformation process has been increased knowledge of partnering — negotiation between equal parties.

New focus

The changed division of roles in the competition for advertisers meant at first a step back to more primitive sales behaviour focusing on insertion prices. This tendency was strongly supported by the media agencies, which often considered a lower price good consultancy.

In order to counteract that tendency, TV 2 Advertising chose to strengthen the expertise of the sales team within the areas of sales and negotiation. Management wanted to differentiate itself from the competitors and maintain the position as the serious supplier who provides the customer with the biggest options in the mix of media and target groups at the same time as managing to provide the most professional consultancy on the choice of media.

'For our competitors and the media agencies, the contact price is the decisive element because it is easy to work with and because it is difficult, not to say practically impossible, to measure anything else', explains the sales director, TV 2 Advertising.

'But when you simplify things that much, you also overlook the customer's needs. And a low contact price achieved by targeting consumers evenly over the entire country is not necessarily the medicine which is best for the customer. That is why we would like to insist that the serious consultancy is of value. And to create a position for ourselves where we continue to be the natural first choice.'

'We do this by focusing on the added values and by being more conscious about the product we sell. We co-operate to a much larger extent than previously with our customers in order to find added values. But at the same time we have become more reluctant to give one-sided concessions. We have become good at giving and taking.'

'The discussion on added values also makes it more apparent to the media agencies that there is some money in it for them', says the sales director.

The new focus has also changed the sellers' jobs. Today they need to be more conscious about the cost price of a spot minute. Previously, the attitude was that the minute price basically did not cost anything, it was in principle free. This attitude has been fundamentally changed. Today the cost price is calculated on the basis of how much it costs to produce or purchase and broadcast TV 2's programmes.

'We were not aware of this earlier. Historically speaking, it was associated with us always having been separated from TV 2 with air-tight shutters. Today both we and TV 2 in Odense have a much greater awareness of the value of the programmes. If TV 2 in Odense presents a skilfully arranged range of programmes and keeps its promises to the viewers, our minutes are worth more. Both with respect to money and value for the advertisers.'

'For the sellers the increased awareness of cost prices and added values also means that there is more focus on the commercial side of their work. There are added possibilities in the organization to sell and create a better income foundation for TV 2 Advertising and thus TV 2. This is why the commercial sides to the co-operation and the negotiation with the advertiser also stand out more clearly.'

At first TV 2 Advertising had a monopoly-like status. It was supported by a fixed price list with very visible discounts. For this reason, the seller's tools were also primarily the dialogue and the consultancy. The new conditions have created a less transparent discount system but also given the sellers more freedom.

'They no longer sit with an open book of discounts, which strengthens them in relation to the advertisers and their consultants, the media agencies. They are now faced with insecurity because they do not know whether others have bought at a lower price. That has always been a nightmare for the media agencies in relation to the other commercial TV stations. They never know whether the others have landed better deals.'

'The many new approaches which the seller can choose between make us more powerful in relation to our competitors and the advertisers but it also provides us with a great potential for creating solutions where an advertiser gets a slightly bigger discount in exchange for a different composition of the advertising package. We can give a bigger discount because we make better use of our advertising blocks in relation to the programming,' explains the sales director.

New demands on the advertisers

If the advertiser is going to get the maximum out of the budget for insertion, it will in the future mean changed demands on the time and the employee and management resources which the advertisers invest in co-operating with TV 2 Advertising.

'Far too often we experience that the advertiser's efforts are used in the creative phase, the co-operation with the advertising agency, while the media plan is entrusted with the media agencies. It is a minimum amount of time, perhaps less than 5 per cent of the time, which is spent goal-oriented on purchase of advertising time. This puzzles me because it is often here that a significant amount of money is spent and here the advertiser can optimize the value of his investment', explains the sales director.

The advertisers justify their deployment of resources by saying that they buy the professional consultancy at the media agencies.

'This means that focus is placed on the contact price and not on the many other areas which may be of crucial importance to whether the campaign will succeed or not.'

The sales director points to the fact that increased openness about the objective of the campaign, the size of the budget and the advertiser's other marketing plans together with the ability to follow up on the consumers' interests are the factors which determine whether the planning of the TV strategy will work.

Distribution and presence are important parameters for achieving success. If the advertiser is not capable of meeting the expected demand, there is a great risk of creating dissatisfaction and bad-will among the consumers.

'If the customer focuses exclusively on contact price, he can easily overlook the other parameters. And then the price can end up being far too high to pay measured by a bad reputation, lack of ability to use the market's interest, upset negotiators and ill-feeling in the organization. It is about finding the optimal mix which uses the possibilities of the TV media in relation to the economic and organizational resources which the advertiser has at his disposal to meet the success parameters', explains The sales director.

'The advertiser who is open gets the best consultancy and the most for his money. Openness in return also makes heavy demands on us. Openness should not result in a buffet table. That is also why our advice may be that the advertiser should forget all about TV spots. Either because his budget does not correspond to his level of ambition or because the advertiser's backing cannot meet the demands that the effect of advertising will create [in which case] we cannot recommend a TV campaign,' says the sales director.

Insight and credibility

The sales director has no doubt about how TV 2 Advertising should use partnering. The open co-operation between the sellers and the advertisers is going to increase the sellers' insight so TV 2 Advertising can act in a way that inspires confidence and credibility in a strong advertising market characterized by competition where credibility is not a hallmark for all actors no matter whether they represent the traditional electronic media such as radio and TV, the new advertising options on the Internet or printed media.

'Our co-operation with TeleDanmark shows the obvious advantages for both parties. We accept a minor bond in exchange for TeleDanmark making a large purchase in the shape of a yearly agreement. This way the advertiser knows that there is airtime at his disposal at the same time as he does not have to make detailed arrangements but can act when the market changes. That is an advantage in a sensitive market characterised by competition,' says the sales director.

The agreement among other things gives TeleDanmark the possibility of making new choices during the year. It may be a change of the mix between TV spots, advertising on teletext and TV 2's internet activities or sponsor agreements without this having any negative influence on the discounts. TeleDanmark can, on the contrary, make maximum use of TV 2's discount systems and also obtain discounts with retrospective application if for instance the number of TV minutes become higher than anticipated.

'This gives us an additional sale without risk of cannibalizing because the turnover is guaranteed already. And the agreement is an advantage for TeleDanmark because our airtime is sold out now. Without the agreement they would have to supplement their advertising in other competitive media with real national coverage.'

TV2 is a fully state-owned corporation, based primarily on commercial advertising as an income. It is the single biggest television station in Denmark, with more than 2 million viewers daily.

TV 2/Advertising is TV 2's sales department. The sale of advertisements is hermetically separated from TV 2's programming in order to ensure a free and independent TV supply. It is exclusively up to the programme department to attract many viewers and preferably the right type – consumers from the target group from the ages of 21 to 50 – which determines the value of TV 2's advertising blocks and thus the price of an advertising spot.

The advertisers, on the other hand, have no influence on TV 2's programme planning. They can only express satisfaction or the opposite by buying airtime in the advertising blocks or vice versa.

TV 2/Advertising employs approximately 90 people whose task it is to sell advertising time, teletext advertisements and look after the development and running of TV 2's website. Income from advertising, which amounted to DKK 1.3 billion in 1999 is the most important source of income for TV 2. Besides income from the sale of advertising spots, advertisements on teletext and www.tv2.dk and sponsor agreements TV 2 receives around DKK 400 million in licence fees.

Appendix 1
The timetable

Set up a diagram which shows what combinations of concessions and compensations are feasible. If you become forced to give in on one point, on what other points and to what extent do you then need compensation? A suggestion as to the design of the diagram can be found on page 203. If you do not have a plan and an overview of where you can bargain, you will end up being defensive which can lead to you making concessions without demanding anything in return.

The diagram is derived from the following analysis.

1. Go over the feasible negotiation variables, times, prices, performances, guarantees, payment plans, hardware, software. Start by making a list of all the variables that may be applicable in future negotiations. Include also the alternatives that may become applicable, e.g. rental instead of purchase.

2. Check what scope for negotiation you have on these points. Can you give more or manage with less? This will give you an impression of the flexibility you have available and the alternatives you can make use of.

3. Find out what consequences it will have for you if you get or give more or less. How will it affect your cost situation if the fixed time of credit is extended from 30 to 60 days? This will give you an appreciation of which points may be sensitive to you and what changes of conditions are less important.

4. Try to analyze what negotiation scope the buyer may have on the different points and if he has more negotiation variables than those you have discovered. In order to achieve that, you have to enter into negotiations or make use of your contacts to find the answer informally.

5. Try to get to know what consequences the different negotiation changes will have on your opponent. If you succeed, you will have a good picture of the variables you can use to create added value and a good idea of how large a part of this added value you have to give away. This picture makes it possible for you to think through where you should remain open and how much you can go into detail when you account for the possibilities you see.

Display your openness with regard to the variables, which are less sensitive and result affected at first. You must be prepared to be open to get more information on the table from the opponent. Without this information, it is difficult to create and make use of the existing added value.

Openness inspires trust. Do not be afraid of opening up before your opponent does. If you keep the negotiations on the theoretical level without disclosing in numbers what a change of condition means to you, you will be in a better position prior to the final zero-sum game. If you keep negotiations on the theoretical level, you can express your interest, the existing possibilities and the direction you are willing to take.

> I promise to see what I can do about the delivery time, it should be possible to reduce it. It may require some extra efforts but I assume that it will be profitable for you anyway.
>
> It, of course, places you in a stronger position if you can deliver more quickly but then there may be several suppliers who want to make use of this possibility.
>
> How much can you save if we can...

While hinting that there may be an opening, you must try to get as much concrete information as possible in return. If the buyer makes his thoughts more specific and tells you about his possible negotiation scope and the consequences which a change would entail, you will have the upper hand when the added value is to be distributed. For a supplier, it is normally better to present a total solution and a cost frame which the customer can accept. For the buyer, it is normally better first to try to put pressure on the total amount, then try to localize the feasible added value and then add it all up in a new package. Then the total amount is put under pressure again during the final negotiation.

It is difficult to know where the opponent is flexible and how big the negotiation scope is with respect to the individual variables. It can be even more difficult to find out what consequences changes will entail. One of the main purposes of the future negotiations is to get this diagram filled out as much as possible. How can you best make use of the contacts you have? How can you phrase your questions in order not to reveal too much about your possibilities at all or too early?

Since most of us have a bad memory, which can make it difficult to get an overview of all the figures in a negotiation, we recommend that you use this diagram as a 'crib' during future negotiations.

Timetable for negotiations

Own situation				The opponent's situation	
Variable	Starting point	Negotiation scope	Effect of change of condition	Negotiation scope	Effect of change of condition
Total					

Timetable for negotiations

Own situation			The opponent's situation		
Variable	Starting point	Negotiation scope	Effect of change of condition	Negotiation scope	Effect of change of condition
Price	1,500,000	1,500,000 down to 1,350,000	**−150,000**		
Payment conditions	10 days net	60 days net	Interest expenditure 10% **Approx. −21,000**		
Delivery time	1 August	1 September	We save + 60,000		
Guarantee	1 year	2 years	Increased risk. Cost increase by **25,000**		
Technical specification	Upon request	Alternative 1: incorporate more Alternative 2: remove demand	Alt. 1: **−10,000** Alt. 2: +80,000		

The sum of all concessions must reach 180,000 maximum.

Appendix 2
Examples of
different strategies

How a buyer sets up his strategy

1. **Keep the negotiation goal in mind. Is it to buy at the lowest costs or to get as much as possible for your money?**

You need to know whether you are interested in the added value at all or whether, due to a short-term lack of money, you need to press the price or the costs down to the lowest possible level or to a level within your budget. Consider whether it really is in your interests to seek the lowest feasible price. You should not let yourself be fooled by a low price, you should look at the totality instead so that the low price does not become eaten up by increased costs somewhere else. There may be a need for internal negotiation with a view to setting up the right goals.

2. **Ask for a new proposition.**

Summon the suppliers you are interested in for final negotiation. Make it clear to them that they do have a chance of landing the deal but that they have competition. Send out a feeler: 'If you want to land the deal you probably ought to look at your proposition again to see what you can do about the conditions. I would like a revised offer from you on my desk a couple of days prior to the final negotiation'.

By making it clear to the seller that he has competition, the negotiation temperature is raised. If the seller does send a new proposition with one-sided concessions, the buyer gets the upper hand psychologically. The one-sided concession may be a sign that the seller is eager to land the deal, that he is insecure of his own position of strength or that he considers this a strategic deal.

If a supplier considers the deal to be strategic, the normal profitability requirements do not apply because he will go to great lengths to get it. How can you argue so that a supplier will consider the deal to be strategic?

The problem is to subject the seller to a reasonable amount of pressure. If you come on too hard, you risk that your proposals will be considered as fight proposals, which is something that often results in negotiations reaching a deadlock. It is therefore an alternative to skip phase two and go directly to phase 3 and try to locate the added value.

An appropriate pressure may be as follows.

- You refer to the existing competition and 'give the seller a chance' to revise his proposition before you meet.

- You say in an anxious tone of voice that the bid does not live up to your expectations.

- You try to make the seller insecure by arguing: 'The money on our budget does not allow this. There is a great risk that management says "no" because it has become too expensive'.

- You ask the question: 'Is this not a deal of strategic importance to you? I believe this is why your competitors make a special effort to deal with us'.

3. Localise the added value.

If you are interested in getting the most out of your money, you have to try to find the added value. If the goal is to buy at the lowest possible price, you should look for the changes which may make it possible for the supplier to lower his price. Make sure that the lower price is not eaten up by other costs somewhere else. In this discussion the so-called timetable may be extremely useful.

Check:

- What variables in the proposition are open to discussion?
- What other variables can you add to the discussion?
- Why are certain variables blocked?
- Can this obstacle be eliminated?

Be active and present your own propositions for change of conditions which are within your allowed negotiation scope. For instance, if you feel you could pay an advance then send a clear signal: 'Provided that you give us a reasonable compensation we can help you finance your costs during the project by means of a considerable advance payment'. It is your job, not the seller's, to investigate what feasible changes of conditions can create added value. If you give him the initiative, he will take the majority of the added value.

By being the one who opens up a bit and signals 'here we can discuss alternatives to help you' the initiative will be yours. The one with the initiative can more easily make the opponent put some of his cards on the table without having to disclose too much about his own position. This gives him the upper hand when the added value is to be distributed. You have a good idea of what the changes are worth to your opponent but he does not have the same insight into your calculations. This means that you do not need to give more away than what it takes to give the opponent an alternative which is better than his second best alternative.

4. Get insight into the seller's prerequisites and calculations.

If the seller returns with a new proposition and presents it as a package in which he has included a number of changes of conditions, it is difficult for you to see what the individual changes entail. In order to make sure that a given change creates added value and saves costs, you should not accept a package solution. You must break up the package. You can do this perhaps by asking: 'If we make use of your new proposition but return to the original delivery time, how will that then affect the price?'

This makes it possible for you to reject the changes which do not result in any gains. If you pack all in one package, it may very well be that the total change is positive but the various pieces of the puzzle both entail bigger gains, costs and risks.

You must also attempt to form an idea of what value a change of condition has for the seller. Has he given in at all and reduced his demand for profitability or has he made a deal which is even more favourable for him? If this is the case, is the division of the created added value then reasonable?

Be aware of the balance between stinginess and businesslike behaviour. You should create an incentive for the opponent to find better solutions. If you cannot do this, your attempts to co-operate will be thought of as pure fight negotiation. A supplier also has to make money.

5. Have a clear idea of how to distribute a possible added value.

If it is your goal to build long-term and stable relations, it is probably easier to accept that the seller also makes a better business and increases his profit. You have to consider this during your preparations, including decisions on the following points.

- How much information about your own situation should you reveal? How open should you be with respect to costs and profit? How many 'truths' should you reveal? If your gain from a change is $100,000, is it then OK to say $90,000?
- Is it a good idea to suggest an incentive agreement, i.e. should the seller have a share of the gains which he is part of creating?
- Where is the line between being naive – businesslike – and greedy when it comes to distributing the added value?
- Should you set a level for the seller within which you can accept a solution? The rest of the profit then goes to him.

6. Test the opponent's limits and make counter offers.

If the opponent fulfils your long-term goals, should you then accept the proposition or take another negotiation round to test the opponent's limits? The possible negotiation gains in connection with a new round should be commensurate with the time and the costs you have to invest in the new negotiations and the annoyance it can create with the opponent. If you want to continue the negotiations, you can follow different routes:

- Should you take a new negotiation round with the other suppliers and give them one last chance?
- What information should you give them? Should you inform them about details of the contents of the propositions, which the competitors have presented? What information can you give about the solutions presented by the competitors? Is it morally defensible to take expertise from a supplier and transfer this to the competitors?
- Should you conduct parallel negotiations, an auction, to raise the temperature of the negotiations? How will that affect the relations?

- Should you forget all about the competitors and make a counter offer instead and thus try the opponent's limits?
- Should your counter offer be negotiable and how clear should your signal of willingness to compromise then be when you make your offer?
- Should you attempt to create insecurity by means of delay and wait and see whether the supplier returns with a better offer?

7. Be forward-looking.

You should avoid ending up in a situation where, sometime in the future, you lack alternatives because, for technical or economic reasons, you have bound yourselves to one supplier. You may need expansion, renovation, technical support or new spare parts. In order to prevent the supplier from being able to take advantage of his monopoly situation at some point in the future, it is important that you negotiate options where it is your right, but not your duty, to let already negotiated conditions continue and to do business.

Alternative strategies for the buyer

Example 1: Outsourcing

A real estate company decides to concentrate its resources on its core business and for that reason wants an external contractor to take over the production of heat and water. In the existing situation the company has its own district heating station operated by the company's own staff. The current expenses to staff and maintenance are $10 million a year. There are statistics for the last 15 years which show how much energy you get out of every ton of oil you use as fuel. There are furthermore statistics which show that operational failures occur for 50 hours on average every year.

It is the goal of the management to press the operating costs down by 10 per cent. The demand for quality which they have set up states that neither the oil consumption nor the operational failures are allowed to increase. A buyer is assigned to sell the operation of the district heating station and the three employees who have operated it.

He contacts a handful of contractors he knows about and asks them the following question: 'Can you and would you be interested in taking care of the operation of our district heating station? The present level of quality must be kept and the payment we can offer you for the operation is about $ 9 million'.

Three of the contractors accept the conditions and the level of payment. An outside observer may think that the buyer has behaved rather naively by putting all his cards on the table even with a proposition of a price level instead of inviting offers the traditional way.

The buyer's purpose with his proposition is not to get some prices and then to give the order to the contractor with the lowest price. His goal is to select a smaller group of contractors who can fulfil the goals which management has set up. He wants to establish a positive relationship with his openness.

The three who have qualified for the final round will be told that they have competition. Prior to the final decision, the buyer will discuss the following.

- The relation between the life and the price of the agreement. By how much can the supplier reduce his price from the $9 million if he gets a deal for more than one year?

- A bonus attached to the consumption of oil. If the supplier can run the plant and achieve a better energy utilisation per ton of oil than in the previous years, a profit will be made. The real estate company is prepared to share this profit provided that the contractor assumes full responsibility for the cost if the consumption of oil should increase.

- A bonus attached to the operational failure. If the supplier can run the plant and reduce the operational failure compared to earlier, there will be a profit. The real estate company is prepared to share this profit provided that the contractor accepts to pay fines if operational failures increase instead.

- Taking over of staff. It is difficult to assign two of the three employees to other tasks within the real estate company. Is it possible for the contractor to offer them employment?

Instead of going for the lowest price, it is about creating a long-term relationship with the contractor who can offer the best solution. In order to encourage the contractors to create added value, you are prepared to share it with them.

Example 2: Purchase of computers

The person in charge of the project has been given a budget of $500,000 to purchase computers and software, and to provide members of staff who are going to work with the computers further training. Instead of setting up a complete requirement specification of all the things you want to buy, the person in charge works out a specification of the non-negotiable requirements. This states the number of computers, the lowest feasible capacity, the programs which must be included, guarantees and access to service. The need for further training is left out at first.

He chooses a number of suppliers with a good reputation and asks them the following question: 'I have $400,000 at my disposal for this purchase, can you accept the demands and deliver at a cost within my budget? If so, I will sit down and discuss the details with you'.

A couple of the suppliers are interested and express that they can accept his demands. These are summoned for negotiations. He makes it clear to them that the choice is between them and a competitor. He says that he is not interested in discussing the price. The $400,000 in his budget must be used. The supplier who can give him the most for the money gets the deal. He leaves it entirely to them to deliver more hardware and software in the total package. In order for them to understand his way of thinking, he says: 'The most important thing for us is not to get the very latest technique or the very latest version of any other programs you would like to add to the package. Maybe you have accessories, which have become off-the-shelf goods and not so easy to sell. If you input them on our computers and if you do not have any direct costs with respect to upgrading, this will become an argument when we evaluate the offers'.

He knows that many suppliers do not consider it very costly to deliver more hardware and software. The costs are furthermore based on the supplier's marginal or own costs. If an enlarged package which has a value of $50,000 to the buyer is calculated to cost $10,000 by the seller, a significant added value has been created. On the other hand, if he demands a price reduction, then you exchange $ for $. Many sellers are less inclined to lower their price than to give more value for the money.

Finally, he gets to the point of further training. 'We have discovered that we will have to give some of the employees who are going to work with the computers some further training'. He states the number of people and the program that they are to be trained in. 'You offer the further training we need but our problem is that we cannot free sufficient funds to send our employees on the usual courses'. Then a long period of silence follows so as to think carefully about this problem. He awaits a possible proposal from the seller. He cannot think of anything so the customer continues: 'Is it not so that when you hold courses there are usually one or two empty places? If we made use of those places, it would not mean that the costs of the course would increase. We will of course pay you for possible course material'.

The seller admits that this is true in itself but that he will not know how the situation is until a very few days before the start of the course. This is not a problem for the customer. His employees can begin with one or two days' notice. The customer is flexible with respect to time as long as all further training activities can be finished within three months. If the seller can accept the proposition, the customer will see whether he can get some more money. This is where the remaining $100,000 comes in. The customer hopes that the supplier will calculate his further training costs based on his marginal costs and not look at his price list. If you let a person have an available place which could not be sold, it does not really entail any costs. Costs in the shape of a lost alternative income will in fact only arise if the customer's only alternative was to buy further training at the normal price.

How a seller can work out his strategy

Determine what the starting point is for continuous negotiations no matter whether it is the present solution, the opponent's enquiry or the offer you have made.

1. Find out what the customer's goals are.

The customer's goals are not identical to his enquiry. An enquiry consists of a mixture of a wish and the non-negotiable demands. The enquiry is often lacking information about the feasible alternatives. For instance, you must attempt to get an answer to the following:

- What does one have to do in order to reach an agreement?
- If you have made a proposition, you must attempt to get a complete counter offer or comments on your offer.
- What is good?
- What does the opponent want to change? Why and how does he want it to be? What needs/problems must be solved?
- How does the customer see himself solving the problems and costs which his demands entail?
- Look at the totality. All the demands for the agreement must be laid out on the table.
- What alternatives does the customer have?

Avoid arguing, listen and summarize and try to form a picture of how the customer has planned it all.

2. Pin the customer down so you can set up a goal to work towards.

Question: 'If I can set up an alternative solution which meets your demands, will I then have a deal?' If you cannot get the goal out in the open and if you cannot read the opponent, he will have the upper hand. Then there is a great risk that you will end up giving more away than needed in order to reach an agreement.

3. Search for the added value.

Here you can use the timetable (see Appendix 1) to help you get answers to:

- What variables in the proposition can be discussed?
- What other variables can you add to the discussion?
- Why are certain variables blocked?
- Can the obstacle be eliminated?

4. Get insight into the customer's prerequisites and calculations.

- What value does a change of condition have for the opponent?
- What will you get in return for accepting a change?
- How should you ask the question in order to get an answer? The buyer is normally not so naive that he answers a direct question and gives himself away. He does not want to give you an advantage prior to a distribution of possible added value.

5. Make it clear to yourself how possible added value is going to be distributed.

During the preparations you have to decide on the following.

- How much information about your own situation should you pass on?
- Should you propose an incentive agreement?
- With distribution, where is the line between being naive – businesslike – greedy?

6. Take a break and analyze the situation before setting up the offer.

7. You present a new total package.

- Try to prevent the opponent from initiating a new negotiation round with the other suppliers. An auction is not to your advantage.
- Should you accommodate to all the opponent's demands?
- Should you make a counter offer to test the buyer's limits?
- Should you indicate that you are willing to compromise with respect to your counter offer?
- Are there other alternatives, which solve the problems?
- Make a new offer. Benefit from the added value you have localized to improve your profitability. If you make concessions, you should

always demand something in return. Consider giving more rather than lowering the price.

- A 'no' does not have to be a 'no'. Even though the customer previously has said no, he can change his mind when he sees the actual offer.

- If you do not succeed in reaching an agreement, you should find out why and what is missing.

- Try to coax a counter offer. Test the limits and do not accept the first best offer that lies within your negotiation scope.

- Do not let yourself by pressured into accepting every deal. The best ones may be those you pass on.

The importance of taking the initiative

Depending on who takes the initiative, even the same negotiation can have different results. A customer has requested an offer with a view to rationalizing his production. Prior to the negotiations, the supplier has presented an offer, which contains the following prerequisites.

- In accordance with your specification we deliver a completely installed machine at a total price of $4,250,000.

- The machine is rated for two-shift work and has a production capacity of maximum 10,000 units per hour.

- Payment conditions: 30 per cent when the machine is produced, 60 per cent after approved installation and use and 10 per cent after the warranty period expires. Fixed time of credit 30 days.

- Delivery time: 10 months from receipt of order.

- We provide one year's guarantee from the time of the first use of the machine.

- The price includes further training and manuals in accordance with your enquiry.

The customer starts the negotiation by explaining that management has not granted means to carry out the purchase. The machine is too expensive. The investment does not correspond to management's demands for payback time.

The seller takes the initiative

'We have to try to find another way of handling the deal so that the demands from management can be met. In order to be able to do this, we have to know by how much the machine is too expensive.'

'You have to lower your price by $400,000.'

(If the customer will not open up and put his cards on the table, you have to keep on asking: 'What order are we talking about, is it 50,000 or 100,000?' If you still do not get any answers, despite a number of follow-up questions, you have to test what reaction you will get with a new offer.)

'If we can find an alternative set up of the transaction which can be put into practice for both parties and which will improve your calculation by 400,000, do we then agree that we have a deal?'

'Yes, provided that the solution you offer meets our requirement specification.'

'First of all we will need an advance payment of $1.5 million. By means of that we can reach better prices on external components.'

'It can possibly be discussed whether you can compensate us for our interest expenditures.'

'What are they?'

'They amount to $90,000.'

'Is it possible to postpone delivery by a couple of months?'

'No, we are making this investment to rationalize our production. If delivery is postponed, our estimated rationalization gain becomes postponed, too.'

'How much money are we talking about?'

'$200,000 a month'

'Then we ought to speed up the delivery instead since quicker delivery is worth $200,000 a month.'

'Yes.'

Now the seller has got the following information on the table:

- The price has to be reduced by $400,000.

- As compensation for an advance payment the customer wants $90,000.

- If the machine is delivered three months earlier, this is worth $3 \times 200{,}000 + 600{,}000$

The seller has not needed to reduce his price to land the deal. Instead he improves his profit by \$160,000 while the customer's calculation is improved by \$400,000. This is possible because an added value is created by means of two changes of conditions, i.e. changed payment conditions and changed delivery time. On account of passive negotiation method on the part of the customer, he does not get any insight into how the changes of conditions affect the seller's situation, he does not discover that the seller improves his profit. If the customer categorically had refused to answer the seller's question, the seller could have tested the matter by presenting two alternatives for the customer to choose between:

Alternative 1: The new proposition as stated above at a price of \$4,290,000. In this there is a moderate raise of the seller's profit. It presupposes that the seller has information suggesting that the customer may be interested in a shorter delivery time.

Alternative 2: The seller sticks to his original offer but goes down to \$4,205,000.

He hopes that the customer chooses the most appropriate alternative, the one with the shorter delivery time. If he is unlucky, the customer will demand both a price reduction and the shorter delivery time.

The buyer takes the initiative

'The machine is too expensive. The investment does not correspond to management's demands for payback time. We have to try to find another set up of the transaction so that the demands from management can be met. If we could pay an advance payment of \$1.5 million, what can you then do about the price?'

'We have to make some calculations. I will return and let you know.'

'I would like an answer now. Do you need a calculator?'

'We can lower our price by some \$100,000.'

'That does not sound like much, I had expected \$150,000.'

'We cannot go that far. Perhaps \$140,000.'

'OK, we will get back on that. How about the delivery time? You have a competitor who appeals to us because of his short delivery time. He promises that he can have the machine ready in seven months.'

'Technically, that is possible but that would mean additional expenses for us which we want compensation for.'

'How much money are we talking about?'

'Around $100,000.'

'OK, let me just recap. With an advance payment you can lower your price to $4,110,000. Quicker delivery costs $100,000 that makes it $4,210,000. If you can give me a discount of 5 per cent, we will end on $4 million and the deal is yours.'

'I cannot go any lower than $4.1 million.'

'Then give me 40 days credit and you have a deal.'

The seller has to lower his price to land the deal. His profit is reduced by some $150,000 at the same time as the buyer besides the price reduction of $150,000 improves his calculation by around $510,000. This is possible because the buyer, and only he, takes the added value which has been created by means of the two changes of conditions, changed payment conditions and changed delivery time. The seller gets no share in the added value because of his passive negotiation method and because of this, he does not get any insight into how the changes of conditions affect the buyer's situation.

These examples show how important it is to take the initiative if it is your objective to get the majority of the created added value.

Conclusion — how to become a better negotiator

An unfortunate proposal can be compared to driving a nail into the wall. It can be done just with one blow but it takes time to pull the nail out again and it cannot be done without leaving a mark where the nail was.

Examples and experiences in this book show that negotiation is a psychological game with high stakes — a game we humans play against one another. Sometimes against opponents whom we know and sometimes against opponents whom we do not know. Do you know yourself? Do you know what affects you in different ways and how you can influence your opponent by varying your behaviour?

If you want to be better at negotiating, you have to start with yourself. Dare to stare your own faults and skills right in the eyes. You can never change your opponents; they are who they are. It is your own behaviour you have to get to know, develop and change. If you are sympathetic and adjust your behaviour to the situation and the opponent, you will experience progress.

Even though every negotiation is unique and calls for its own solutions, there is a lot you can learn from other people, trades and situations. Compare and dare question what you do. Discussions are not dangerous. Discussions are there so that we can get to know one another better, gain respect for one another and get new information on the table. As a skilled negotiator, you know that it becomes much easier to reach an agreement, if you can create added values, and to negotiate about the distribution of these added values even if the negotiation amounts to nothing more than a zero-sum game.

We have described a number of negotiation tools in this book. Some are honest while others are debatable. If you try to make the negotiation into a game where you constantly try to shine by being superior to the opponent — well, then we have failed in getting our message across. If you think that negotiations must be won by fighting and clever tactics, then we have also failed. On the other hand, if you choose not to use more negotiation strength then the situation calls for in order to achieve your goals and you manage to land a deal with two satisfied parties, then we have succeeded.

You have to learn to use the tools. The best training comes from negotiating a lot and by gaining experience. Our examples show that we can learn a lot from the negotiations, which we all participate in every day.

Do you need a facilitator or consultant to make your negotiation and partnerships a success?

Companies with different interests, visions and targets very often need a supporting assistance helping guiding them towards success. When an otherwise progressive negotiation hits a road block or gets diverted it helps to have someone to redirect these negotiations.

In many of the negotiations and facilitations assignments we have been involved in, we find the greatest hurdle to be that of trust. The two parties don't trust each other, but find it easier to adapt to a neutral facilitator.

These are the obvious and tangible reasons to appoint a consultant or facilitator. But even more important is that a facilitator, can increase the possibilities to bring out and emphasize the impact, visions and common goals.

Another important skill of the facilitator is that he just wants the job done. He is not involved in feelings or other personal related issues during the negotiations. He is not to keen on the process, but focuses primarily on the final result.

The skilled facilitator and consultant operates in the big pictures and has plenty of experience dealing with mergers, negotiations and added value.

Partnerships cannot thrive without an experienced negotiator.

Very often we as facilitators encounter the traditional attitudes to doing business, and this can occasionally be the greatest showstopper.

Last, but not least, ask the facilitator for references. A good facilitator often multiplies his own salary by X? The professionals can prove this.

We wish you good luck with your negotiations and the creation of added values via the partnership concept.

If you have comments on this book or you would like to make contributions to it, you are very welcome to contact us at one of the addresses mentioned below or by e-mail.

UK and International
MarketWatch Management Ltd
211 Piccadilly, London W1J 9HF. UK.
Tel +44 020 7917 2924; Fax +44 020 7439 0262;
website www.marketwatch-management.com;
e-mail mail@marketwatch-management.com

Denmark
MarketWatch Management ApS
Bredgade 36, DK-1264 Copenhagen K.
Tel +45 33 36 07 77; Fax +45 33 36 07 78;
website www.marketwatch.dk;
e-mail mail@marketwatch.dk

Sweden
AB Förhandlingskonsult AB
Artillerigatan 8, 3, 114 51 Stockholm. Tel +46 8 662 1006;
e-mail iwar@forhandling.com

The MarketWatch organization specializes in negotiation technique, consultancy before, during and after negotiations, definition of added value and training in and seminars on negotiation technique and related communication under the concept name *Communicative Competence*.

About MarketWatch Management
"Getting results through credibility, balance, and innovation"

A single dynamic, independent, network organization, with a strong basis in the Nordic reference platform works to motivate and promote business growth of companies across functions, industries, and interest organizations.

The organization focuses exclusively on its core concerns: Negotiation Technique, Communicative Competence, and consultancy in those fields.

MarketWatch Management is headed up by Keld Jensen who has 15 years of experience in the fields of management and negotiation. All the way from smaller enterprises to companies quoted on the Stock Exchange as a generator of ideas and CEO contributed to the development of people, projects, and products; he has taken part in due diligence, business acquisitions, and disposals, which has put him in a position to further develop his human resource concepts.

Most recently, through his activities in MarketWatch Management, Keld Jensen has contributed to books on Negotiation Technique, published on the Scandinavian and international markets: *The Negotiation Manual, Partnerships and Negotiation Techniques*; he has acted as a business consultant and trainer to a broad spectrum of leading Scandinavian and Danish organizations.

MarketWatch Management is, together with its Swedish sister corporation AB Förhandlingskonsult and CEO Iwar Unt, widely recognized as a leader in its field worldwide, with publications and clients from China to the US, and has very stringently defined ethics, a factor that allows the company to reach documented, high-quality results.

Index